re Designs

DATE DUE			

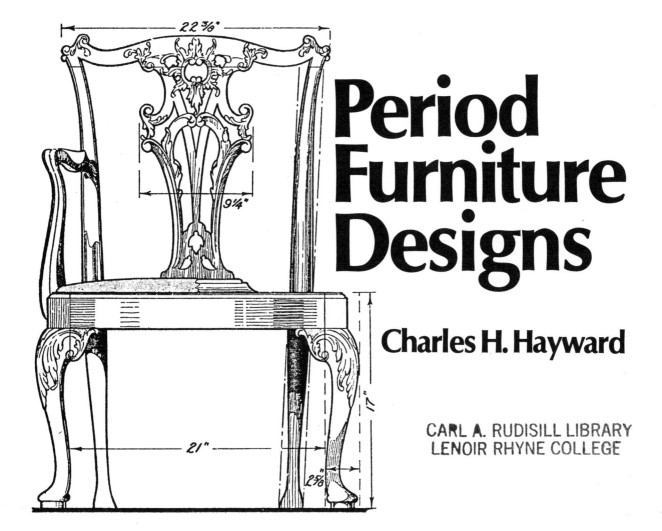

Period Furniture Designs

Charles H. Hayward

 Sterling Publishing Co., Inc. New York

Published in 1982 by
Sterling Publishing Co., Inc.
Two Park Avenue
New York, N.Y. 10016

ISBN 0-8069-7664-0

Library of Congress Catalog Card No.: 82-50557

First Published in 1956, revised edition
in 1968

Published by arrangement with Evans
Brothers, Ltd. This edition available in the
United States, Canada and the Philippine
Islands only

Printed in U.S.A.

Contents

Foreword

Much of the furniture created in previous centuries has a charm and dignity largely lacking from most of the mass-produced and machine-made furniture of today. No doubt this is mainly responsible for what seems to be an ever-increasing rise in the popularity of old pieces. Of course, they have a scarcity value and many consider period furniture to be a better investment than the more conventional stocks and shares in the present uncertain economic climate. Certainly 'antiques' generally continue to command higher prices each year. But whatever the reasons for a person's interest in old furniture —aesthetic, pecuniary, fascination with its history, or intrigue concerning the gifted techniques of designer and craftsman—it is hoped that this book will be found to be of value. The drawings originated as a series appearing in the *Woodworker* magazine. They proved so popular that it was decided to publish them in book form with additional drawings and information on construction. The latter is obvious from an examination of the furniture itself, in many cases, but it is not always possible to be absolutely certain about how a piece was made short of the scarcely practicable method of breaking it up to find out. In these cases the author has given the usual method found in other similar pieces of the period. Anybody who has had much experience in the repair of period furniture knows that by the eighteenth century certain methods of construction had been generally adopted. For instance, the lapped-dovetail form of construction for furniture carcases was used everywhere with adaptations to suit the details of the design. At the same time to be dogmatic is to ask for trouble. The unexpected turns up from time to time, and you find a form of construction which you have never come across before.

It is impossible in a book of this size to give more than a few representative types, and we are conscious that there are many omissions. We have, however, endeavoured to make the range as wide as possible both in period and type. Those who want to make reproductions will find the general details useful, even though they do not find the actual pieces they would like to make. We have included on pages 91 to 97 plates showing the progression of various pieces, partly for their interest, and also because they show the general types of furniture that would have been made during the various periods.

This new edition has been extensively revised and redesigned and some additions made to provide a wider coverage of the periods from which examples are selected.

We should like to thank all who have been kind enough to give us permission to take measurements and details of items in their possession.

Oak Stool Late 15th century

Of its kind this stool is most attractive. The proportions are excellent, and, despite its solid construction, the effect is extraordinarily rich. The carving is a delightful piece of design and, being pierced, looks light and even fragile, though in fact it is extremely strong as its survival after nearly five hundred years can testify. It consists of four parts assembled dry. A rail passes through the uprights and is held by wedges. The uprights are tenoned into the top, the tenons being lightly shouldered at the sides, and pass right through the top as indicated in the upper illustration. The top has a circular carved centre *motif,* pierced except for a bar left along the middle. The latter is rounded at the underside and serves as a convenient carrying handle. Each upright is pierced and carved in a Gothic design, one different from the other. To

lighten the effect the wood is hollowed away inside opposite the carving so that the tracery of the bars is considerably thinner than the thickness of wood as seen at the edge ($1\frac{1}{4}$ in.). The rail carving is especially effective, this again being pierced and, for its period, is delicate. The stool has suffered considerable damage, though for its age it is well preserved. One upright has been patched at the inside where it has apparently been split away, and some of the carving has been broken away in parts. Its survival since the late fifteenth century, however, is a tribute to its sound construction and good design in placing delicate detail where it is not likely to be exposed to hard usage. The drawing suggests the wear inevitable in its long life, but the actual breakages are not shown. The stool is of Norman origin.

Drawn from the original in the Victoria and
Albert Museum, South Kensington

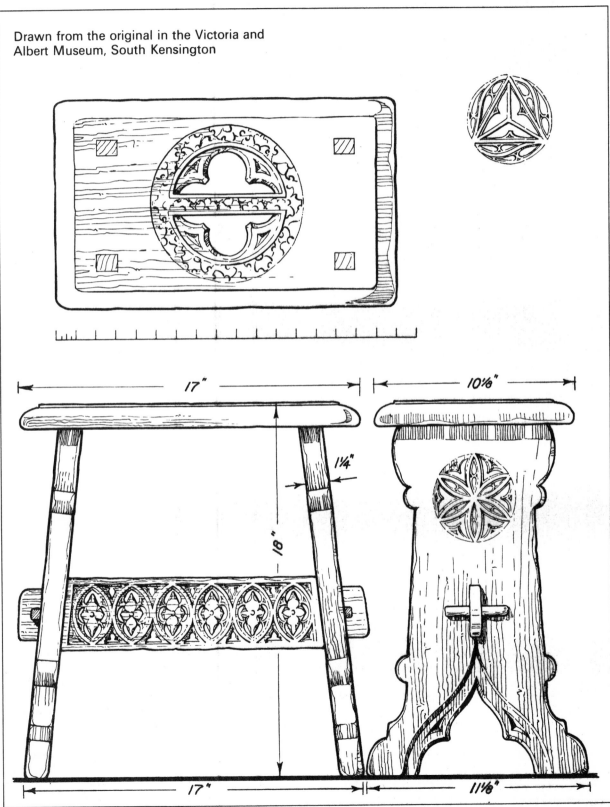

Oak Chest Early 16th century

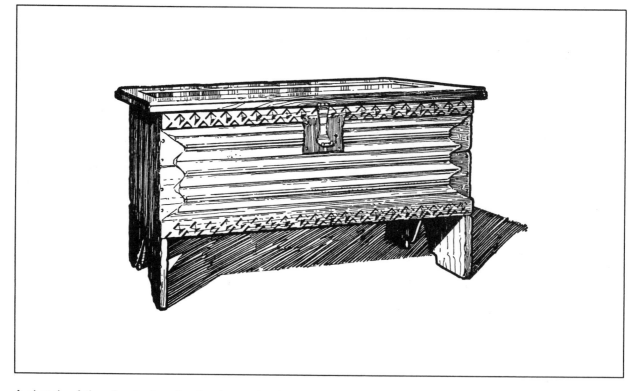

A sketch of the chest, showing its decorative front. The lid has practically no overhang front and back

This is a good example of an early planked chest. As the term suggests, it consists of a series of boards nailed and sometimes pegged together. A chest constructed in this way has an inbuilt weakness in that the front and back are liable to split because the planks are rigidly fixed to the ends, the grain of which is upright. As they are about 14¾ in. wide, shrinkage is inevitable; the rigid fixing resists this hence the split.

The linenfold motif and strapwork carving are deeply and vigorously cut, and the result is an attractive if somewhat crude chest.

At the left-hand end is a shallow trough with sloping side. The method of hinging is primitive, consisting of metal eyes joined by a link. The grain of the bottom runs along the length.

Drawn from the original in the Maidstone
Museum and Art Galley

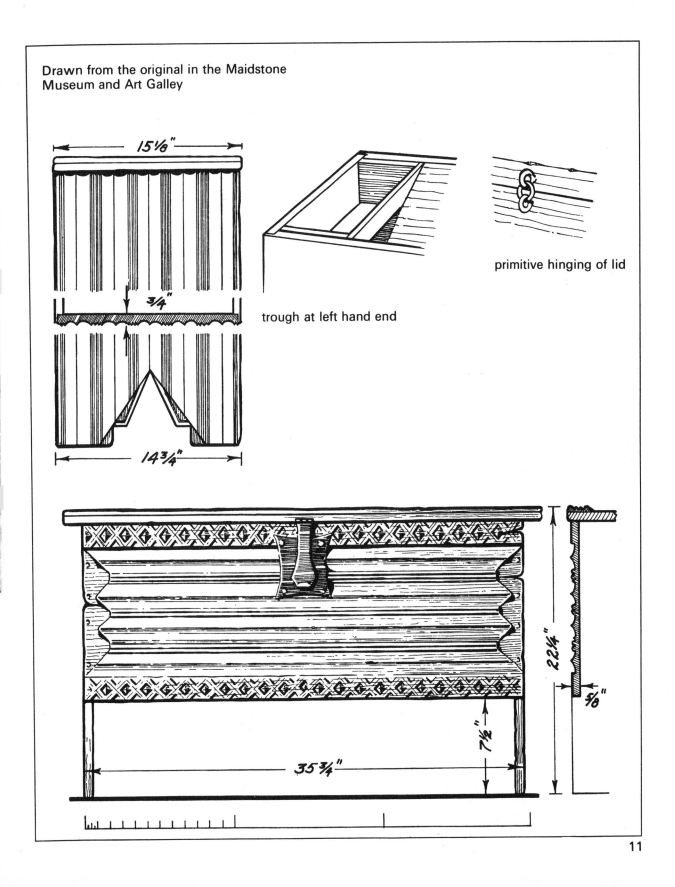

15⅛"

¾"

14¾"

trough at left hand end

primitive hinging of lid

22¼"

⅝"

7½"

35¾"

Oak Draw-table Early 16th century

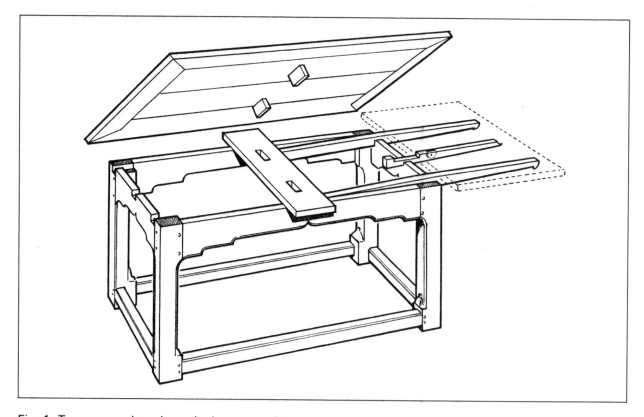

Fig. 1. Top removed to show the bearers and levers

The leaves are supported on tapered bearers which raise them to the level of the main top when extended. The main top is free to rise to allow the movement, but side play is prevented by vertical pieces which are tenoned beneath the main top, and pass through slots in the centre fixed piece between the leaves. To enable the main top to be raised when the leaves have to be closed a lever (see drawing) is depressed. This is pivoted on a projection tenoned beneath the leaf. Its use saves having to bend right over the leaf to reach the main top. One of the bearers is now missing.

The main framework is put together with pegged mortise and tenon joints. Stops fitted to the bearers prevent their being pulled completely out. The heaviness of the legs is reduced in an ingenious way by continuing the curve of the rail into them, thus reducing the section to $2\frac{3}{4}$ in. square at the middle.

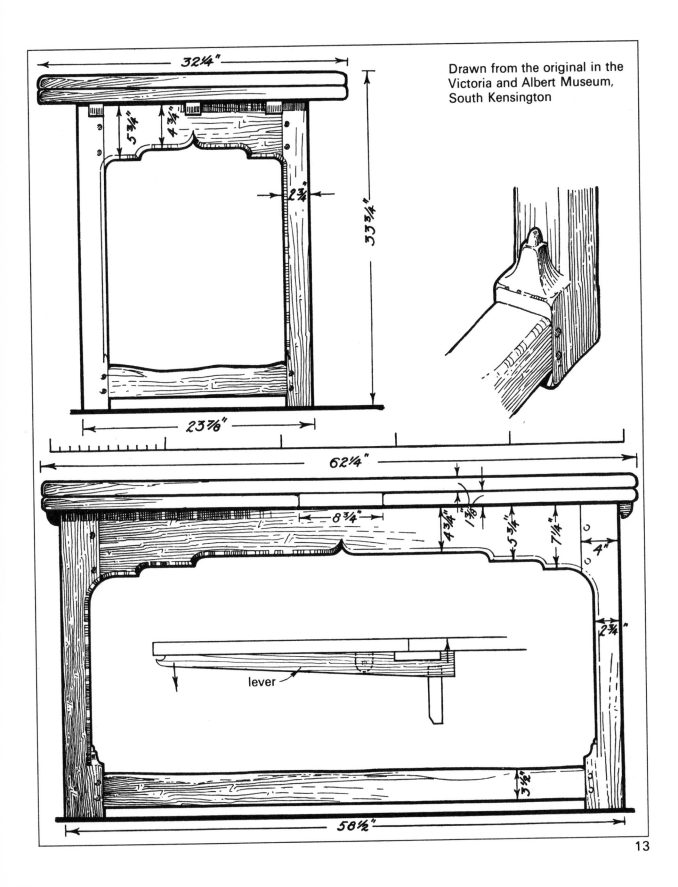

Drawn from the original in the
Victoria and Albert Museum,
South Kensington

32¼"

5¾"

4¾"

2¾"

33¾"

23⅞"

62¼"

8¾"

4¾"

1⅜"

5¾"

7¼"

4"

2¾"

lever

3½"

58½"

Framed Oak Chest About 1600

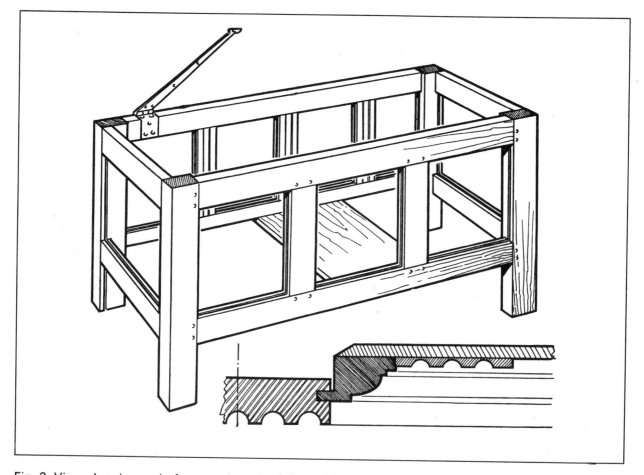

Fig. 2. View showing main framework, and enlarged plan section through panel. Mortise and tenon joints are used for the framework, and the edges are grooved. The panels themselves do not fit in the grooves. Instead the applied moulding is tongued in, giving the deeply recessed effect.

The main structure is framed together with mortise and tenon joints. The maker would appear to have used a plough for working the panel grooves because the last named are continued down into the legs in some cases. Why some were stopped at the bottom mortises is something of a mystery. Perhaps the craftsman intended all to be stopped and gave the legs to an apprentice to groove for him, and only realised when they were half done that the apprentice had taken those he had finished right through. One wonders what punishment the unhappy lad received.

Alternatively the craftsman may have had a plough with the cutter set near the front. If he then chopped the mortises first the front of the

plough could run out into them.

An interesting feature of the panels is that the arcading is applied, the grain running horizontally, whereas that of the panels and the pilasters is vertical. The section in Fig. 2 shows the construction. The actual panels are quite thin—no more than $\frac{1}{4}$ in., and the large moulding carved with egg-and-tongue is applied and is mitred round. This moulding has a projecting tongue, and it is this which fits into the framing grooves. The panels themselves do not enter the main framework at all. Presumably the panels must have been dried thoroughly before the moulding was added because they would be liable to split in the event of shrinkage since they are held by the moulding glued across

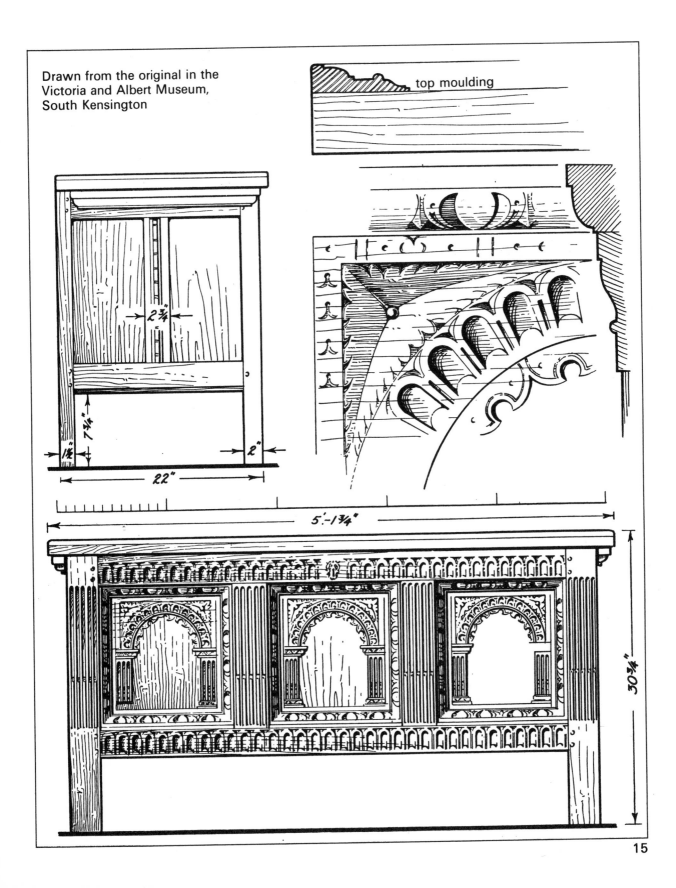

Drawn from the original in the
Victoria and Albert Museum,
South Kensington

top moulding

2¾"

7¾"

1½"

2"

22"

5'-1¾"

30¾"

the grain. In fact one of the panels has split, but the other two appear quite sound despite this somewhat unorthodox treatment.

In most panelled chests of this type the panels fit directly into grooves in the framework, their edges being chamfered at the back to suit the grooves. An exception is when the panels have raised carved detail as in the case of the linenfold panel or the curved rib type. In these the panels are flat at the back and rebates worked at the front to enable them to fit into the grooves.

The chest bottom consists of five boards fixed in rebates at the bottom, the grain running from front to back. A small trough or edged shelf is fitted at the left-hand end immediately beneath the top. Cranked strap hinges are used for the top. The latter has cross-pieces fixed beneath at the ends, and there is a moulding mitred round at the top. This has caused splitting owing to shrinkage of the wide top and its being held rigidly by the cross-pieces and moulding.

In the present case the arcadings of the panels are sawn by hand and carved, but it is interesting to note that at Aston Hall, Birmingham, the long gallery is lined with arcaded panels which must number somewhere in the region of a thousand. A quick way of producing these was devised as a close examination reveals. They were in fact made on on the lathe. A single moulded ring was turned and cut through to make two semi-circular arcadings. It is an interesting early example of seventeenth century mass production.

Oak Bed End First half 16th century

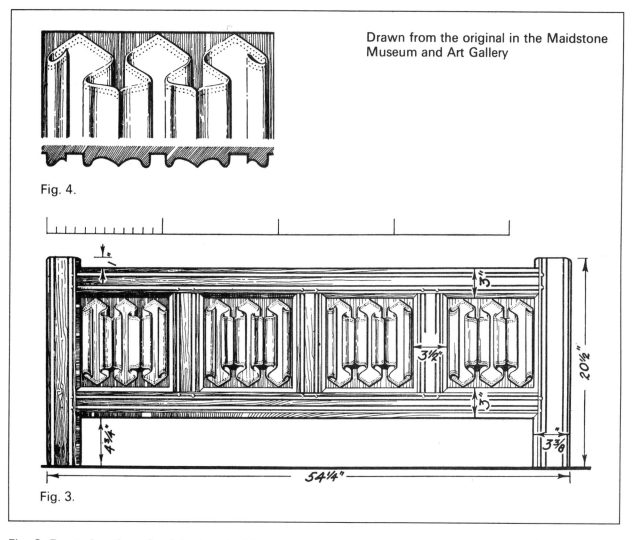

Drawn from the original in the Maidstone Museum and Art Gallery

Fig. 4.

Fig. 3.

Fig. 3. Front elevation of oak bed end with linenfold panelling

Fig. 4. Linenfold panel detail

An interesting detail of construction is that all the chamfers around rails and uprights are scribed rather than mitred. This means that the front shoulders, instead of being square, are at an angle so that they align with the chamfer. The appearance is identical with the mitre. Panels are grooved in, and the reduction to enable them to fit is made at the front so that the linenfold device stands forward. Fig. 4 gives details of this. Note the vigorous character given to the work by the folds shown in the section. The

hollows are not just evenly balanced shapes, but are taken in deeply near the outer folds. The channelled moulding along the framing members is a form of flat bead, and was probably worked with the scratch stock. This rather delightful bed end could be made up and used today in conjunction with a modern divan. It is just the right size for a double bed, though a single one could be made up to have three rather than four panels. The panel widths could be altered accordingly.

Oak Side Table First half 17th century

Fig. 5. Construction of the table framework

For its size this table is heavily built and somewhat crude considering the amount of timber that has gone into its construction.
It offers comparatively little accommodation.
It will be seen that the front legs are planed so that the mortised surfaces are at right angles with front and canted rails, enabling square shoulders to be cut.
Panels fit in grooves, and the last named must have been largely chiselled or scratched since they are stopped at the joints. The cupboard bottom fits in grooves about $1\frac{1}{4}$ in. up from the bottom. The top is pegged down, and the moulding worked around the edges. This was apparently worked with a moulding plane since the path of the tool can be seen across the corners. The section has a rather deeply indented quirk at the top, and the craftsman could not have realised the effect of this when taken right across.

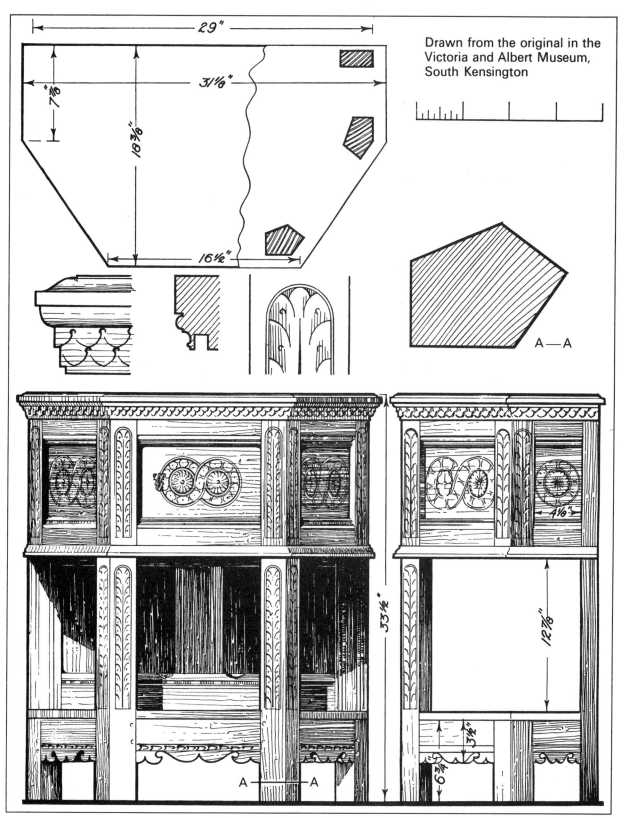

29"

31⅛"

7⅞"

18⅜"

16½"

Drawn from the original in the
Victoria and Albert Museum,
South Kensington

A—A

33½"

12⅞"

4⅛"

3½"

6¾"

A —— A

Oak Gate-leg Table 17th century

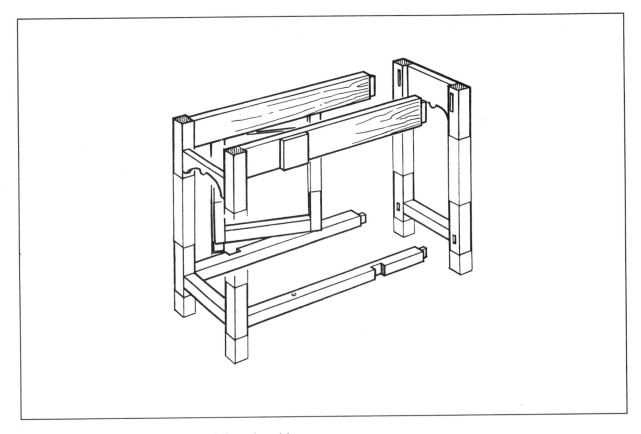

Fig. 6. Main framework showing joints. In tables
of this kind there are usually two rails at the
drawer end. In this example there is no top rail
and no sign that there ever was one.

This interesting piece is in oak throughout, and
is a good example of a design which still
remains popular after three centuries. It would be
as useful today as when it was made. There is a
drawer at one end which fits between the
shaped spandrel rail and the top, and the other
end is similarly shaped and carved though it
does not open as a drawer. The top and its
leaves are modern replacements; the originals
may have had square edges or they may have

been moulded. It will be noticed that the
scrolled feet were originally built out, but the
applied pieces have since been knocked off.
The main framework is put together with mortise
and tenon joints assembled dry and pegged. The
mortises generally meet in the thickness of the
legs, the tenons being cut away at an angle at
the ends, thus having maximum length. The
carving is of a quite crude nature, being mostly
of the V-incision type with little modelling.

20

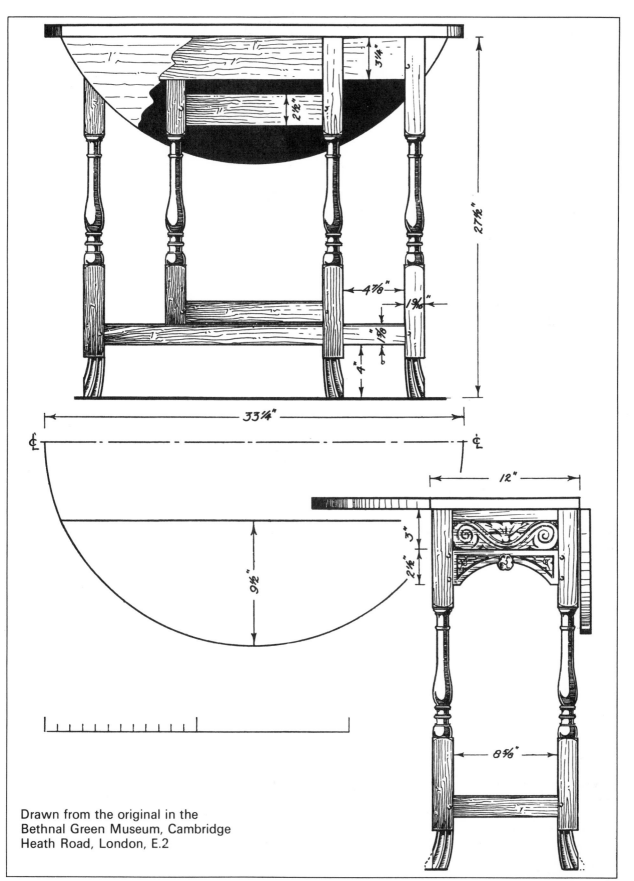

3¼"

2½"

4⅞"

1⁹⁄₁₆"

1⅞"

4"

27½"

33¼"

9½"

12"

3"

2½"

8⅝"

Drawn from the original in the
Bethnal Green Museum, Cambridge
Heath Road, London, E.2

Oak Welsh Dresser Early 18th century

The term 'Welsh Dresser' is used in the trade to describe a type rather than to denote country of origin. Many of these pieces had shallow cupboards built into the upper portion. Oak was widely used, though later specimens often had mahogany (generally in veneer form) used side by side with oak. In this example the main show parts are of oak, but the shelves, drawer sides, backs, and bottoms, and bottom shelf are of elm. A moulded facing is applied to the edges of the upper portion, this being mitred at the intersections, and stopped short above the shaped portion of the ends. The back is of oak boards, and at the bottom is a curious boxed-forward portion (see dotted lines in side elevation) presumably for display purposes. Drawers have a cocked bead let into a rebate, and a similar bead is added to the bottom edge of the carcase.

The upper dresser portion is put together with housed joints. The grooves run right through to the front and are concealed by the applied moulding. Sloping grooves in the shelves enable plates to rest up against the back. It will be

22

seen that the moulding of the shelves overlaps both at the top and the bottom, presumably to give a thick appearance. There seems to be no practical reason for it since the plates rest in the sloping grooves. It certainly makes dusting extremely awkward, though in an age of ample service this did not matter much.

Back and sides of the lower portion are solid, and are tenoned into the legs. Top front rail is dovetailed, but the lower portion beneath the main drawers is largely an imitation. The small side drawers are real, but the centre one is a dummy, the centre leg running up behind it and finishing beneath the centre top drawer. It has a form of bridle joint. A rather unusual feature is that the bottom front stretcher rail runs right through and is halved to the centre leg. Drawer runners are provided, but there are no dustboards. Drawers are dovetailed, and a cocked bead is fitted all round.

It is interesting to note this farmhouse type of furniture in oak was widely used at a period when walnut was employed for fashionable furniture in the towns.

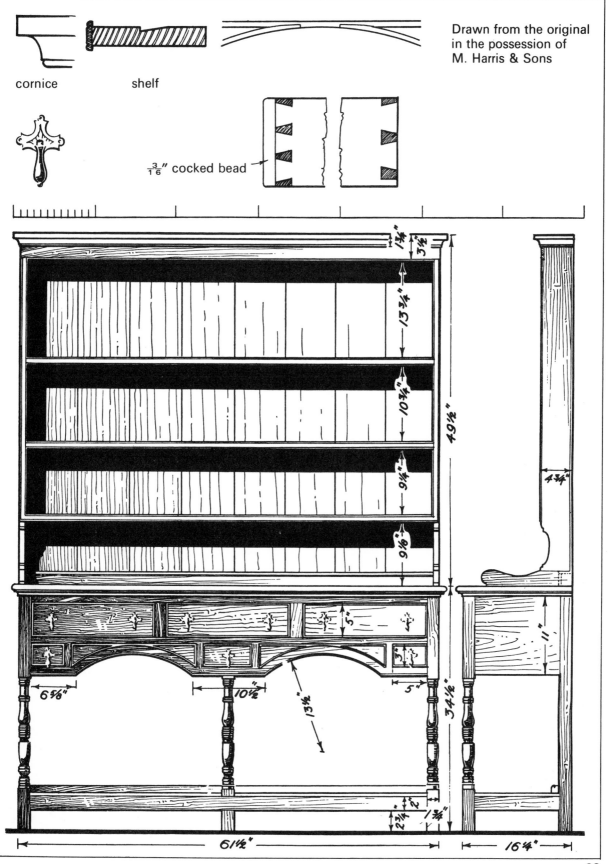

cornice   shelf

Drawn from the original
in the possession of
M. Harris & Sons

$\frac{3}{16}''$ cocked bead

1¾"
3½"
13¾"
10¾"
9¼"
9½"
49½"
4¾"
5"
3"
11"
34½"
6⅝"
10½"
13½"
5"
2¾"
2"
1¾"
61½"
16¼"

23

Oak Cradle 17th century

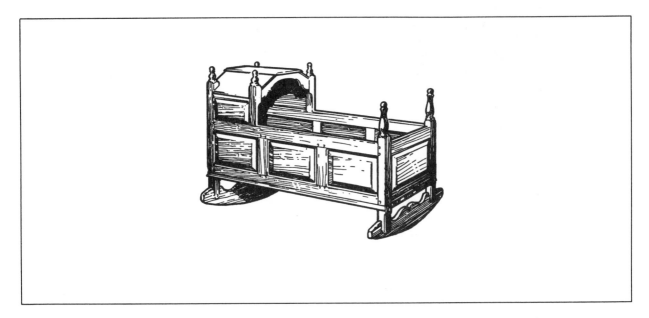

Fig. 7. Sketch of the cradle

All show parts of the cradle are of oak, but the bottom, which consists of boards laid in crosswise, is of elm. The main structure is made up of corner posts, turned at the top as shown, with rails tenoned into them. These rails have a simple thumb moulding worked at the inner edge; also the intermediate uprights. The panels are fielded. A form of bridle joint is used where the corner posts join the rockers. The cradle is interesting in that it shows typical details of the period. It will be noticed that the thumb moulding of the rails is taken right through, being cut back locally at the joints and mitred. This is shown clearly in Fig. 8. As it would be impracticable to work the moulding along the length of the corner posts, a simple stopped chamfer is worked opposite the panels only.

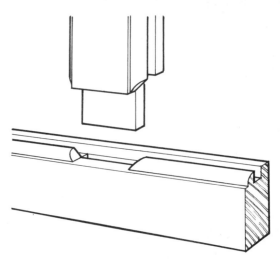

Fig. 8. How the moulding is cut back and mitred opposite the uprights.

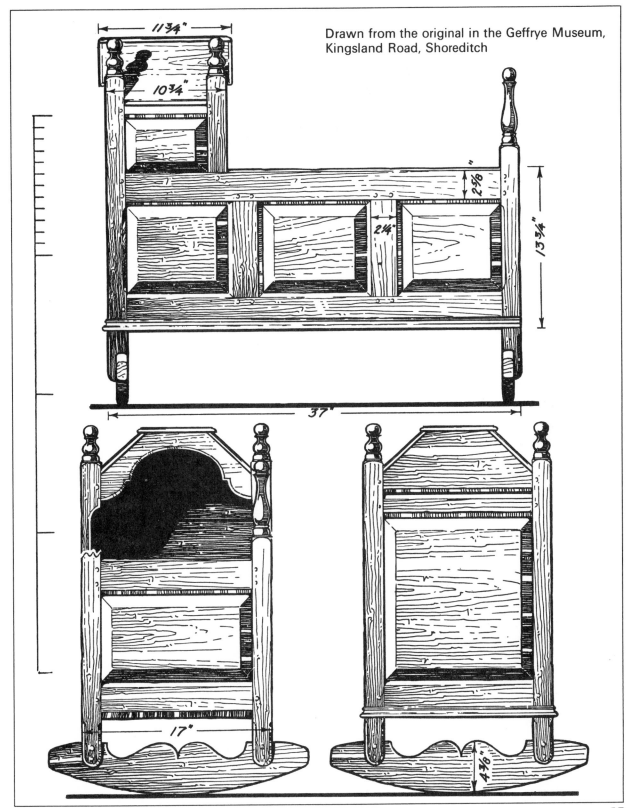

Drawn from the original in the Geffrye Museum, Kingsland Road, Shoreditch

11¾"

10¾"

2⅝"

2¼"

13¾"

37"

17"

4⅛"

Oak Chair Yorkshire About 1660

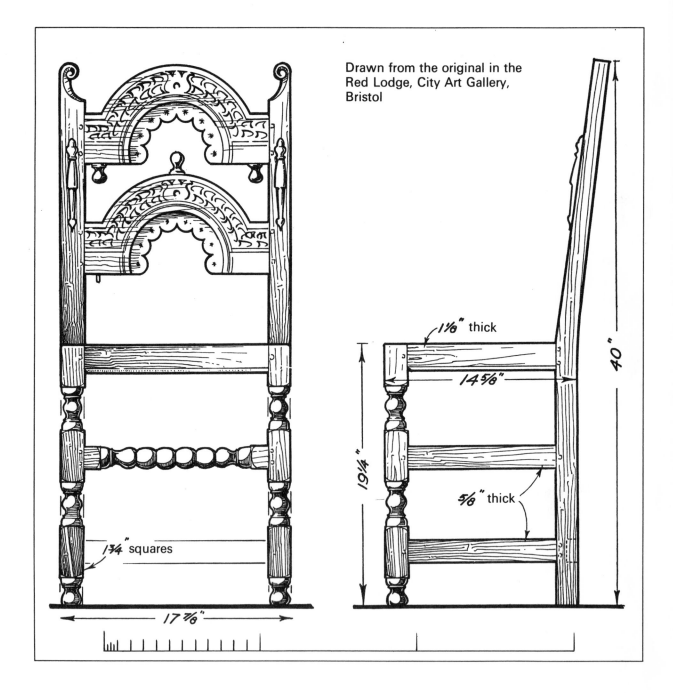

Drawn from the original in the Red Lodge, City Art Gallery, Bristol

1⅛" thick

14⅝"

5⁄8" thick

19¼"

40"

1¾" squares

17⅞"

A type generally known as the Yorkshire chair. It was probably the earliest chair to have an open back, previous specimens having the back panelled. The turned pendants and finials are a typical feature; also the shaped back rails, and

scrolled ends to the back uprights. Most chairs of this kind had a solid grooved-in seat, this being set a little below the seat rails. A shallow recess was thus formed in which a squab cushion could rest.

26

Oak Chair Commonwealth 1649–1660

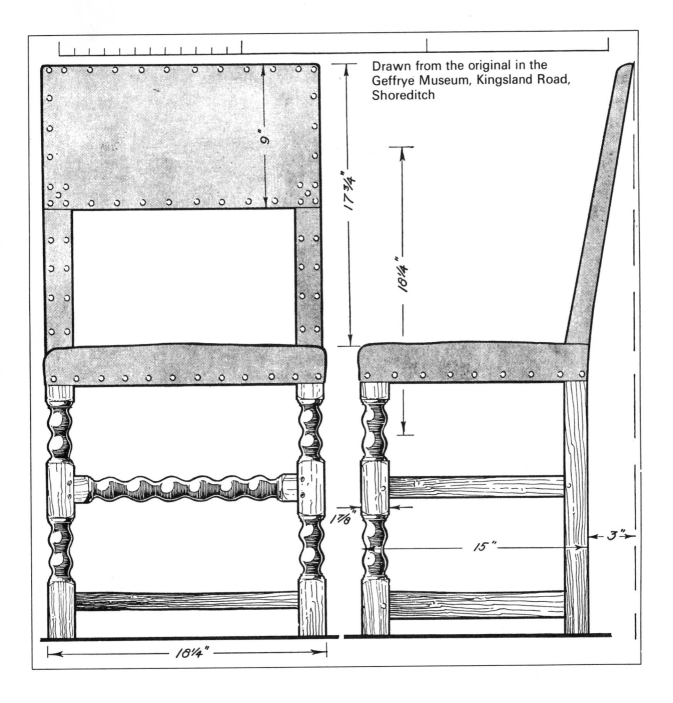

Drawn from the original in the
Geffrye Museum, Kingsland Road,
Shoreditch

9"

17¾"

18¼"

1⅞"

15"

3"

18¼"

The chair is in oak with the seat and back
covered with leather. Metal studs are driven in
around the edges of the covering, these being
arranged to give a decorative effect. Legs and
stretcher are bobbin-turned from squares
finishing 1⅞ in. Note the absence of any rake

to the back legs. The turned stretcher and plain
rails level with it are tenoned directly into the
legs. There is no back stretcher at this level.
At the bottom the side and back stretchers
enter the legs, but the front one is set in and is
joined to those at the side.

27

Oak Stool 17th century

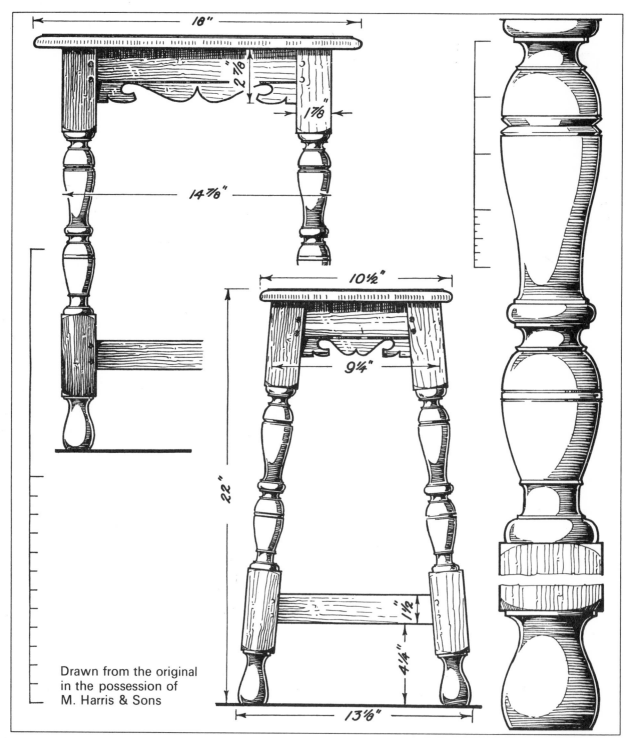

18"
2 7/8"
1 7/8"
14 7/8"
10 1/2"
9 1/4"
22"
1 1/2"
4 1/4"
13 1/8"

Drawn from the original
in the possession of
M. Harris & Sons

Typical stool of the period. Although square in front elevation the legs are splayed at the ends to give stability. The portion occupied by the shaping of the top rails has a sloping rebate worked along it. The inner corners of the

squares forming the legs are taken off and an interesting note is that this was apparently done before the legs were turned, because it runs across the turning in some of them, forming a flat.

28

Walnut Chair Mid 17th century

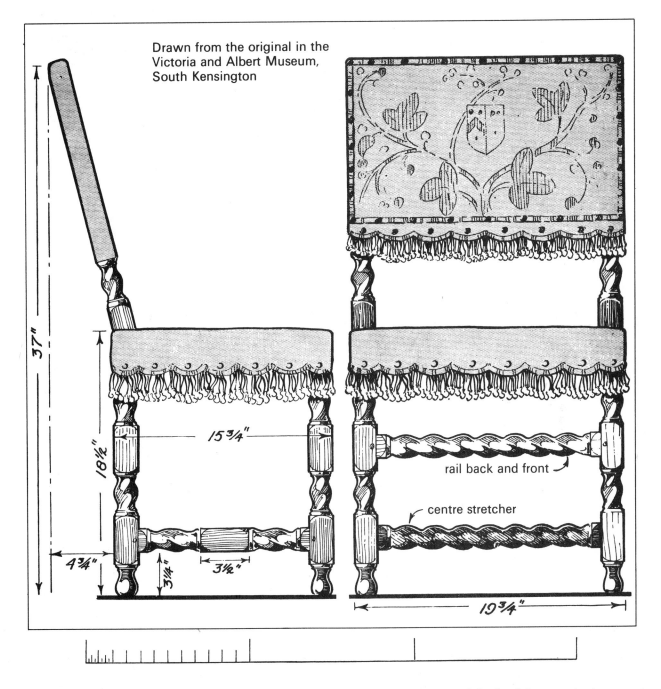

Drawn from the original in the Victoria and Albert Museum, South Kensington

37"

18½"

15¾"

4¾"

3¼"

3½"

rail back and front

centre stretcher

19¾"

A point about the chair that immediately strikes one is that, although the back slopes at a pronounced angle, there is no rake to the back legs. It was not until the second half of the seventeenth century that it occurred to the chair maker that to splay the legs backward would give increased stability, though an early attempt to get over the difficulty is to be seen in some early seventeenth century oak chairs in the packing out of the back legs at the bottom. The seat and back are covered with tapestry finished with a decorative fringe at the edges. There is, of course, no springing. The latter did not come until the nineteenth century. The following sizes may be of interest. Legs and turnings are from $1\frac{5}{8}$-in. squares. Top back rail is 4 in. wide; that below it $1\frac{1}{2}$ in. wide. Seat rails are $1\frac{3}{4}$ in. wide.

Carved and Gilt Mirror About 1715

Fig. 9. Two simplified designs based on the mirror shown opposite. The mouldings alone could be gilt, or the whole thing could be in polished wood. The glass for these mirrors might be 20–24 in. high. The smaller size makes them more suitable for a small room.

This mirror is of fine proportions and workmanship. A feature of special interest is that the flat surfaces are in polished walnut (veneered on a pine groundwork). The mouldings and detail are carved and gilt. Around the mirror is a narrow bevel. Such a mirror would look well in a large and fairly lofty room or hall. In a small room it would probably

appear too big, and we give in Fig. 9 suggestions for two simplified smaller frames. The same general design is followed, but elaborate detail is omitted, and the smaller size makes them suitable for the average small room. The whole thing would be made up as a complete frame put together with mortise and tenon joints, veneered, and with the mouldings planted on.

From the original in the
possession of
M. Harris & Sons

9"

3"

6½"

3'-5"

4'-8¾"

14½"

21¼"

33¼"

31

Walnut Corner Cupboard Early 18th century

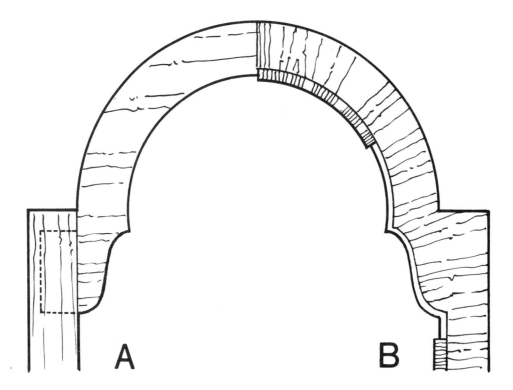

This is walnut veneered on an oak groundwork. In common with almost all Queen Anne work the grain of the veneer runs crosswise. The same thing applies to the cornice moulding, which is built up of cross-grained strips of walnut glued to a softwood or oak groundwork. The moulding of the bars is built up similarly. To strengthen the latter the usual plan was to veneer the back, the grain running lengthwise. This in fact was the first operation. Strips of walnut with the grain running crosswise were jointed together to give the length, and the back veneered. The flat rounded section was worked and the moulding separated from the strip. This is shown at (A) and (B) Fig. 28 on page 108. The curved portion of the cornice moulding joins the straight part with a curved mitre.

Unless this is done the members will not coincide on the joint. As the curve is circular, the moulding was probably turned, and, it is an interesting thought that, a second cupboard was likely to have been made using the other semi-circle. It may still be in existence, though it is possible that the moulding was used for an entirely different piece. Shelves are in line with the horizontal bars. In this cupboard they are straight at the front, but it was common to give them the double ogee shaping shown in the alternative.

Fig. 10. Method of making and veneering the doors. Framing joints are shown at (A) and the appearance after veneering at (B).

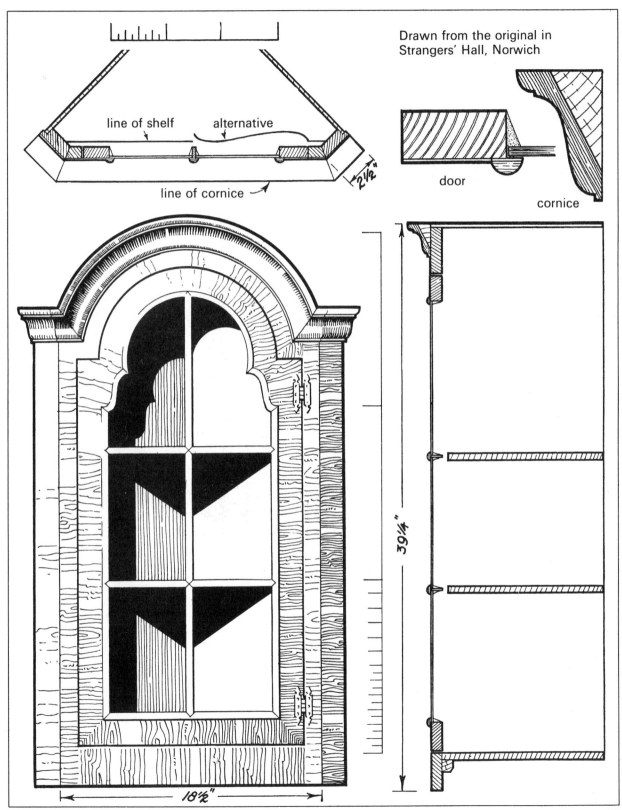

line of shelf   alternative

2½"

line of cornice

Drawn from the original in
Strangers' Hall, Norwich

door

cornice

39¼"

18½"

Walnut Bureau on Stand About 1715

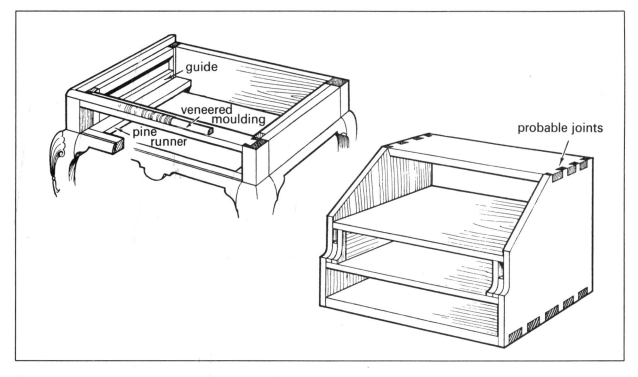

guide

veneered
moulding

pine
runner

probable joints

Fig. 11   View showing construction and probable joint details. The carcase is veneered
after being assembled. Rails have the grain running crosswise. The large centre rounded
moulding is veneered. Small mouldings of the period were often worked in the solid, cross-
grained wood being glued to a straight groundwork.

This small bureau is well proportioned. The
legs are particularly well shaped, having the
high knee and restrained curvature which makes
for dignity and avoids all suggestion of
bandiness. They are in walnut, as are also
the drawer sides, backs, and bottom. The main
carcase is walnut veneered on pine, the rails
having the grain running crosswise as in nearly
all Queen Anne furniture. Certain parts are in
oak; drawer fronts (veneered), lopers, and the
shaped front rail of the stand. The latter has an
applied facing of walnut with the grain running
across. This fashion for having the grain running
crosswise is even carried to the cocked beads.
Because the carcase is veneered it is impossible
to tell the exact form of the joints, but chips in
the veneer reveal that through-dovetails were
used, and their probable form is suggested in
Fig. 11. The veneer is of about the thickness of
present-day saw-cut veneer. The legs have
squares at the top, side and back rails being
tenoned into them. The top front rail is
lap-dovetailed in. Note that the ear pieces are
continued across between the legs as a rail, and

have an applied walnut facing to enable the
curve to be worked.
An interesting but not altogether happy feature
is the special shape of the back legs. Clearly
they were made to this flat shape to enable the
bureau to stand close up to a wall, but the
resulting shape is not altogether pleasing. In
any case it does not completely surmount the
problem since the skirting would prevent the
carcase from making a close fit up to the wall.
At some period in its history the bureau has
been unskilfully repaired, patches of veneer have
been laid without regard to the original form.
Some have been taken right over the cross-
banding and herring-bone inlays. The brass
knobs are not original, and were probably
Victorian replacements of brass drop handles.
Incidentally the small right hand drawer in the
stationery nest is not original, and a note
pencilled on the underside of the bottom states
that it was replaced on October 4th, 1832. One
wonders where and by whom. It has almost
become an antique within an antique, so
to speak.

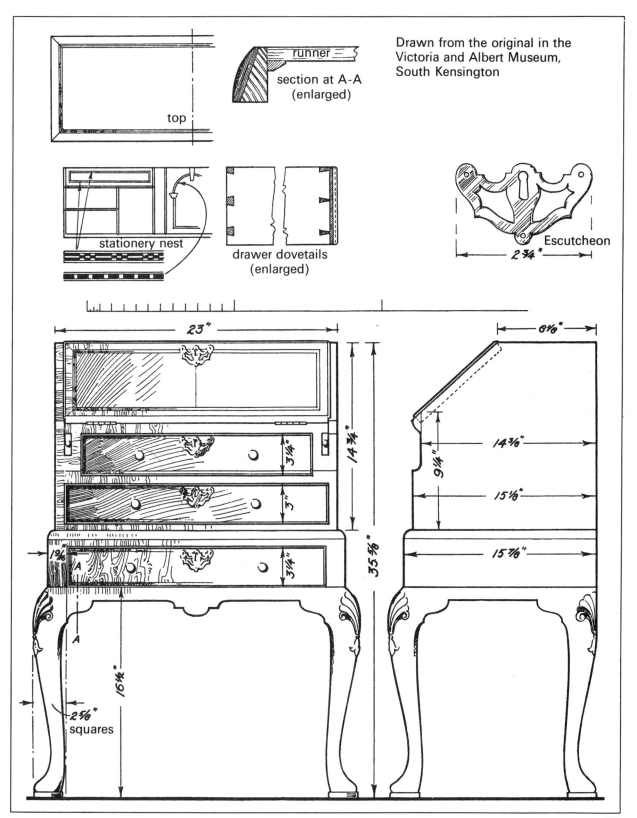

top

runner

section at A-A
(enlarged)

Drawn from the original in the
Victoria and Albert Museum,
South Kensington

stationery nest

drawer dovetails
(enlarged)

Escutcheon

2 ¾ "

23 "

6⅛ "

3¼"

14 ¾ "

14⅜"

9¼"

3"

15⅛"

35⅝"

1⅜"

A

3¼"

15⅞"

16½"

A

2⅝ "
squares

Walnut Stool Early 18th century

The stool is in walnut with a cross-grain facing applied to the lower part of the rails, this enabling the curvature of the legs to be continued around the sides. Thus the wide rails replace the more usual ear pieces. The cabriole legs are of specially fine shape with shell carving on knee and scroll beneath the rails. The spade foot is worth noting. It is made entirely by carving and is well modelled with deep curved recesses cut in at each side (see plan). Immediately above each recess a tapering hollow is carved, this running out to nothing at the ankle. This makes a decorative feature in itself, but that is not its entire purpose. Its main reason is that it reduces and softens what would otherwise be a steep and rather ugly increase in the line of the foot. The appearance would be that at A. The dotted line shows how the hollow modifies it. The seat, of course, has no springing. The latter did not come into use until the nineteenth century. The stuffing is supported by webbing beneath the hessian.

36

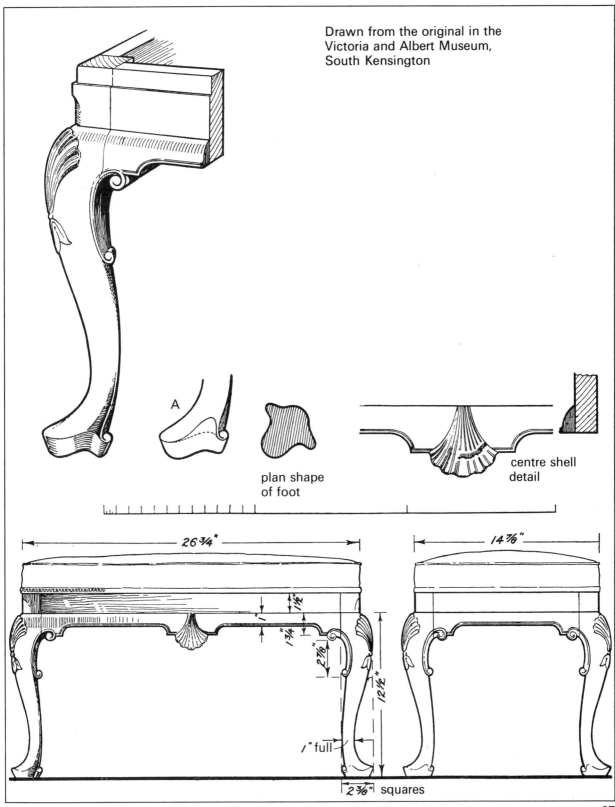

Drawn from the original in the
Victoria and Albert Museum,
South Kensington

A

plan shape
of foot

centre shell
detail

26 ¾"

14 ⅞"

1½"

1"

1¾"

2⅛"

12½"

1" full

2⅜" squares

Walnut Chair, Cabriole Leg Early 18th century

Although solid walnut is used for the shaped parts, the back uprights are cross-veneered on the flat front surface. An interesting feature of the construction is that side and front rails are not tenoned into the front legs. Instead the rails are halved together (see plan) and the legs tenoned up into the frame so formed. The vast majority of normal chairs are made by tenoning (often with a haunch) the seat rails into the legs. Usually there is no difficulty, the mortises (or occasionally the tenons) being at a slight slope to allow for the splay of the rails. In some Queen Anne chairs, however, this is awkward in that the plan shape of the seat is curved. There are no angular front corners, the whole thing taking the form of a continuous sweep as in the present example. To enable the rail shoulders to be square the top rectangular portion of the leg would have to be cut down considerably as at A, Fig. 12. This would mean a loss of strength in itself, but in addition there would be little wood left in which the mortises could be cut. In fact only a roughly triangular shape would be left, involving restricted tenon length. Furthermore the shape of the rails would make a great deal of cross grain unavoidable. Still, this sytem of construction was sometimes followed, and the craftsman got over the difficulty by fixing stout inside brackets (see shaped part at A, Fig. 12). These had the effect of binding the two rails together. Since the brackets might be anything up to 2 in. thick the strength was sufficient for the job.
The awkward form of construction must have been realised, however, and this, no doubt, was the reason for the alternative method by which the front and side rails were halved together, the shape cut in them, and the leg either tenoned or dovetailed up into the frame so formed. The dotted lines at B, Fig. 12 show the squares of timber required to enable the shape to be worked, and it should be noted that the inner shape is plotted so that the thickness is considerably greater over the legs, so avoiding much loss of strengtn owing to short grain. Fig. 12, C shows the first stage in which the parts are halved together, and the rear shoulders marked round. In practice the craftsman probably cut and fitted the rear tenons first as it would be awkward to fit them after the frame was assembled. After cutting the tenons the halved joints would be glued up as at C and, the glue having set, the shape sawn out as at D, Fig. 12. Some chairmakers preferred to cut tenons at the top of the legs, and corresponding mortises had to be chopped in the frame. Others cut a dovetail shape as at D, Fig. 12, and formed a notch to receive it in the outer surface of the frame as shown by the dotted lines. In either case the dovetail or the tenon passed right across the halved joint and so served to bind it together.
It will be realised that all these Queen Anne chairs were cross-veneered around the rails, and this hid any unsightly joints. The top moulding forming the rebate for the loose seat was either planted on the top edge, or was let into a rebate worked around the edge before veneering.

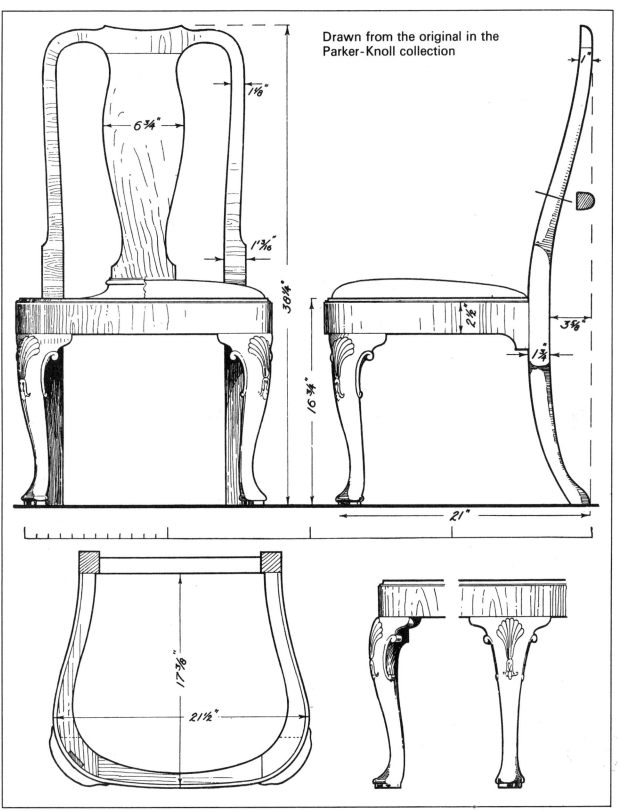

Drawn from the original in the
Parker-Knoll collection

1⅛"

6¾"

1"

1³⁄₁₆"

38¼"

2½"

3⅝"

1¾"

16¾"

21"

17⅜"

21½"

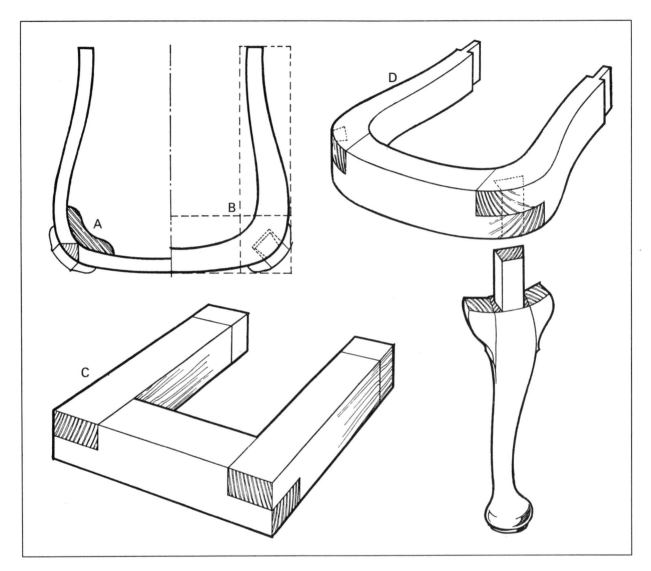

Fig. 12. Chair construction of the Queen Anne
period. A. Tenoned construction. B. Halved
frame method. C. Halved joints before shaping.
D. After shaping and ready for jointing to legs.
Both tenoned method (A) and halved
construction (B) were used.

Mahogany Wall Mirror First half 18th century

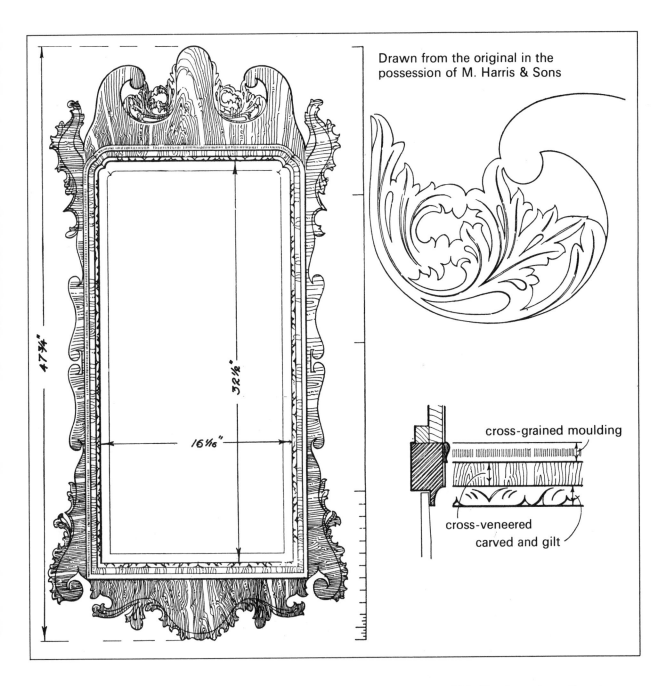

Drawn from the original in the possession of M. Harris & Sons

cross-grained moulding

cross-veneered

carved and gilt

This mirror is of special interest in that it shows a transition of styles between the Queen Anne and the Chippendale periods. The moulding surrounding the frame is cross-grained, a typical Queen Anne detail, and the shaped and indented top corners are a feature frequently found in woodwork of the early years of the eighteenth century when walnut was still fashionable. At the same time the wood is mahogany, and this did not come into general use until about 1730. The fretted scroll and leaf work, too, suggest a later period. The probable date is about 1730–40.

The entire shaping is fretted out of mahogany veneered on pine and is decorated with V-incised lines. These are cut with carving tools. It should be noted that the two repeat scrolls in the middle of each side are not original but are an addition probably made during repairs at some period.

Mahogany Chair About 1755

Of its own particular kind this is one of the finest chairs ever made. The workmanship is of the first quality, and there is a sense of proportion and subtlety of line that only a really capable designer-craftsman could produce. Every detail is 'right'. The cabriole legs are dignified, with high knee, restrained curve, freedom from bandiness, and gradual taper from knee to ankle. The back legs have a delicate compound shape, and appear to change in accordance with the angle from which you view them, and the splat is a rich piece of design which, apparently fragile, is in reality surprisingly strong.

It is an excellent example of how beauty can be won from the technicalities of a craft. Consider the back legs. Their compound curvature at first makes it difficult to see how they were schemed in a piece of timber. Yet the setting-out reveals it as shown by the broken lines at the right-hand side. Each back leg needs a piece of wood of $4\frac{1}{2}$ in. wide to enable the side sweep to be cut in it, whereas the whole of the front curvature needs only a width of $1\frac{3}{4}$ in. The latter is really a most remarkable economy of timber and is possible owing to the whole leg being made to slope inwards towards the floor. This limitation of width imposes a restriction on curvature, and in consequence we have a delicate, refined

shape, free from all extravagance, a characteristic of good woodwork. Much the same applies to the front legs, which need a total thickness of no more than $2\frac{5}{8}$ in. to enable the shape to be worked.

The seat rails are rebated to take the loose seat, which is a simple webbed frame. A serpentine curvature of about $1\frac{1}{4}$ in. extent is given to the front rail, which is of about $1\frac{1}{8}$ in. thickness. Thus, a $2\frac{3}{8}$ in. thickness would be needed to work it. The top back rail bows backwards to the extent of about $1\frac{1}{4}$ in., and the centre portion is taken off at an angle at the front, as shown in section in the side elevation.

Matching the armchair are two plain dining chairs. They are identical in detail except that the width is 22 in. instead of about $24\frac{1}{2}$ in. over the squares, and the over-all seat depth is $19\frac{1}{4}$ in. instead of $21\frac{1}{4}$ in.

A chair of similar design appears in Chippendale's *Director*. The back is almost identical, but the leg carving is different, and French scroll feet are used instead of the turned club foot in the present chair. There appears to be no direct evidence of the origin of the chairs, but clearly so fine a specimen could only have come from a first-class firm of cabinet-makers such as that of Chippendale.

42

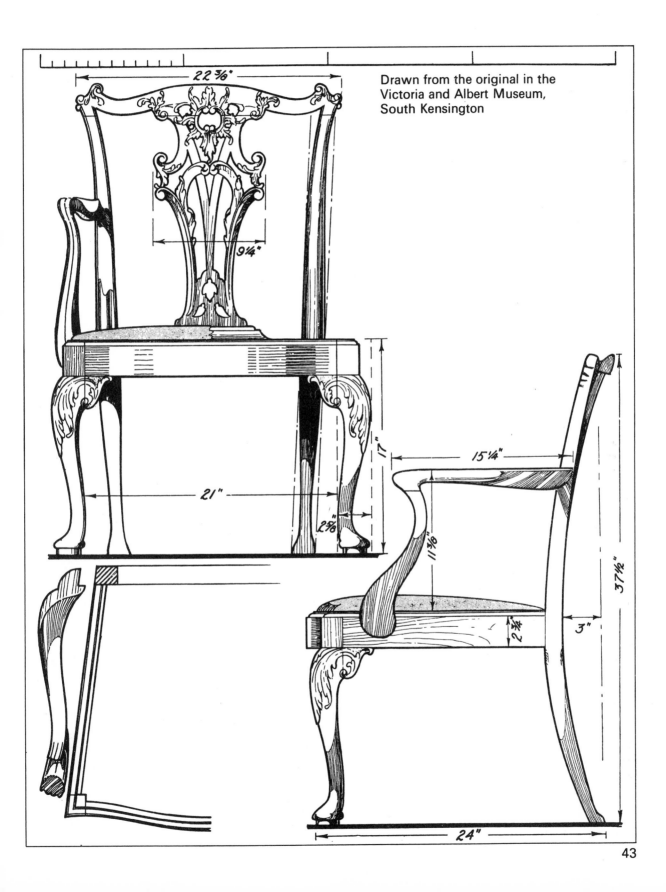

22 ⅜"

9¼"

Drawn from the original in the
Victoria and Albert Museum,
South Kensington

17"

21"

2⅝"

15¼"

11³⁄₁₆"

37½"

2¾"

3"

24"

Mahogany Bureau Bookcase About 1750

This interesting piece is 3 ft. 6 in. wide over the bureau, and 3 ft. 4½ in. over the bookcase. All show work is in mahogany, drawer sides, backs, and other semi-show parts in oak. Drawer bottoms, backs, and so on are of pine. The cornice is made up as a complete, separate unit and is held in position by blocks. Its moulding is backed with pine, and a dentil fret is planted on the face of the wide square member as shown in the enlarged detail. It is omitted in the scale drawing as it is too small to show clearly.

An interesting feature of the doors is that there appears to be only one centre stile. In fact the stile of the left-hand door is concealed behind the other, the two being counter-rebated so that they fit together flush (see section).A rather unusual triple section is used for the door mouldings. At the intersections they are enriched with carvings.

Beneath the fall is a large stationery nest with the usual drawers and divisions, these being of a rather more severe pattern than usual. All drawers are dovetailed together, and have cocked beads around the edges. Handles and escutcheons are brass and show French influence.

Construction of the bureau carcase is given in Fig. 13. The top is lap-dovetailed in, the joint

being concealed at the top by the applied moulding. The latter is shown in the enlarged sections on page 47, from which it will be seen that the bookcase carcase drops inside it. A more satisfactory method would be to make the moulding wide and rest the cupboard upon it. It would save damage to the narrow edge of the moulding. All drawer rails are tenoned in. The fall is clamped at ends and top, the corners being mitred. Bracket feet are made up independently, the front ones being mitred, and the back ones lap-dovetailed. All are screwed in position and have glue blocks rubbed in the internal angles.

The upper carcase is lap-dovetailed together, and grooves are worked from front to back to receive shelves. Doors are put together with mortise and tenon joints, and it is clear that the sloping rebates on the meeting stiles expose the tenons. In practice the doors would be assembled normally and the sloping rebates worked afterwards. The tracery of the doors is made up of a back bar with mouldings applied to the face. The curves are worked in the solid. The cornice is a separate framework consisting of a square-edged frame veneered on the face. The moulding has a softwood backing and is mitred round.

Drawn from the original in the
possession of the Society for the
Preservation of Ancient Buildings

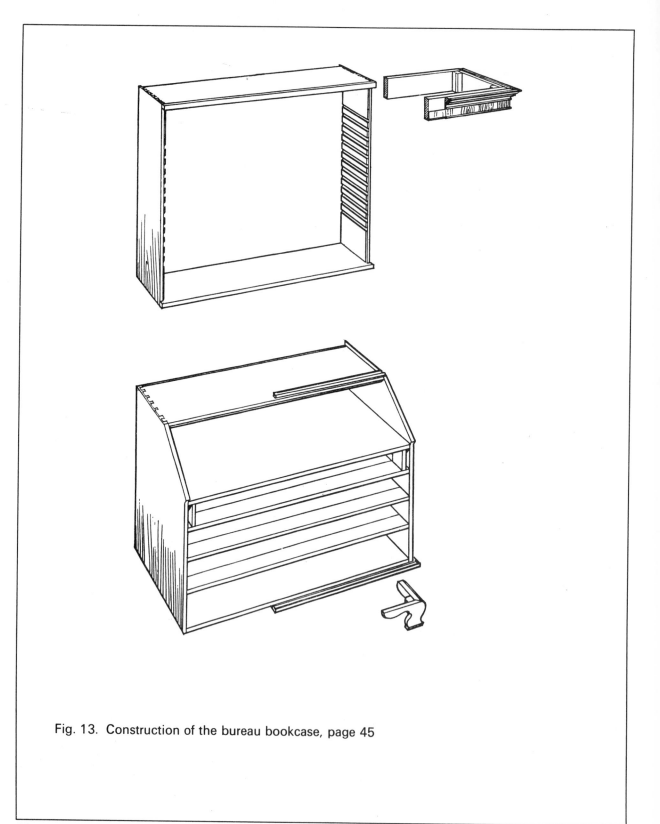

Fig. 13. Construction of the bureau bookcase, page 45

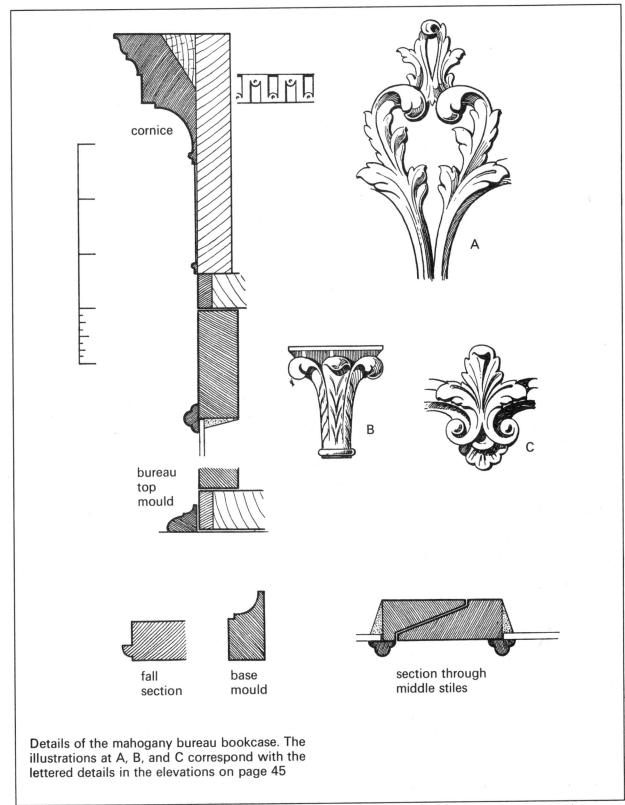

cornice

bureau top mould

fall section

base mould

section through middle stiles

A

B

C

Details of the mahogany bureau bookcase. The illustrations at A, B, and C correspond with the lettered details in the elevations on page 45

Mahogany Tripod Table with Piecrust Edging
Chippendale Period

This delightful type of occasional table was popular in the mid-eighteenth century. In the best tables the top was always cut in the solid. The centre part was recessed on the lathe and the edging cut in by the wood carver. To cut a top cleanly was extremely difficult because of the awkward grain necessarily encountered in parts. In cheap replicas this piecrust edging is made up as a separate item and glued on. By this method it is made on the spindle moulder, but it is not as satisfactory because, apart from its liability to become loose, the spindle moulder cannot reach into acute corners so that the true section is not followed into the corners.

The present table top is cut in the solid, and is pivoted so that the table can stand out of the way when not in use. A metal catch on the underside holds it rigid or releases it. An interesting feature is that it is also free to revolve. This is effected by the swivelling double collar which fits over the top of the main pillar. The lower collar has a hole right through it to enable

it to slip over the pillar, whereas in the top one the hole goes half-way through only. A wedge tapped through the upright prevents it from being lifted off, but does not interfere with its revolving action. It will be realised that the two cross members beneath the top serve to stiffen the latter across the grain. They are fixed to the top with counterbored screws. In the case of a modern copy of the table it would be advisable to bore extra large holes to allow for possible movement due to shrinkage.

The legs are slot-dovetailed to the centre pillar, and a specially made metal strap is screwed on beneath to resist the inevitable strain. These dovetails were invariably tapered in their length so that the fit was quite loose until the joint was practically home. This made the fitting much simpler as it was easy to tell where any over-tightness occurred. The spiral of the pillar and the acanthus leaf work are beautifully carved, and the claw and ball feet are vigorously modelled.

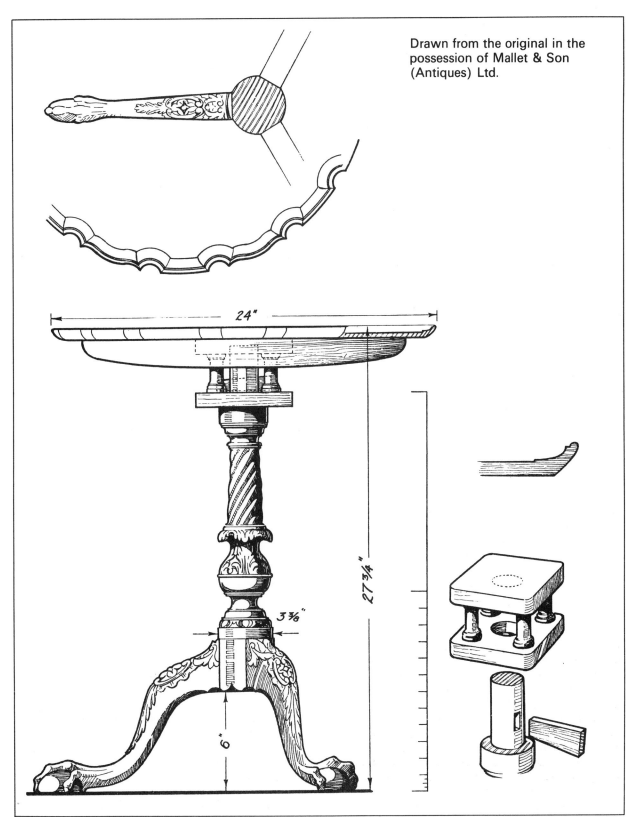

Drawn from the original in the
possession of Mallet & Son
(Antiques) Ltd.

24"

27¾"

3⅜"

6"

Mahogany Card Table Mid 18th century

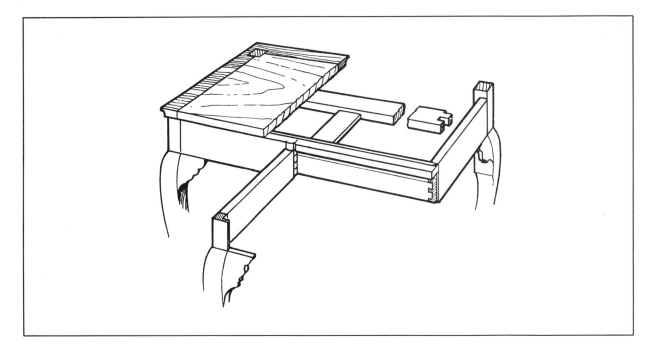

Fig. 13. Cut-away view showing how table is made. It is difficult to say exactly how the top (which is felt covered) is fitted, but an examination suggests that the front legs pass through, or at least into it. It is edged as shown, the grain at the ends being in the same direction as that of the main panel.

A feature of special interest is that, in the extended position, the table can be used either for cards or for dining. There are two hinged tops. When the upper one is opened, a polished surface is revealed; when both are opened the usual green baize appears. To make up for the difference in level the rail of the hinged leg is provided with a pivoted support, which can either be raised as shown on page 51, or folded away level with the rail. Card table link hinges are fitted to both tops so that there is no projecting knuckle at the top. The legs are

especially graceful, and have been cut from $2\frac{1}{2}$ in. squares (without the ear pieces). The illustration in Fig. 13 shows the construction. Three of the legs are fixed, all the rails being tenoned into them. At the odd corner the back rail is lap-dovetailed into the side rail. The swinging rail is tenoned into its leg, and is pivoted to the main table framework with a knuckle joint which enables it to move through 90 degrees. At the middle of the framework is a centre cross-rail dovetailed in. A cocked bead $\frac{1}{8}$ in. wide is fitted around the drawer.

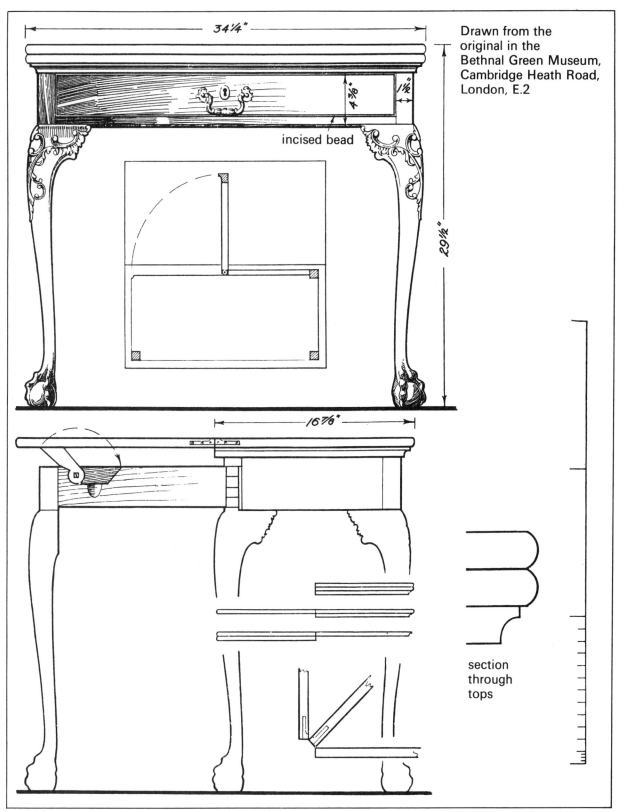

34¼"

Drawn from the
original in the
Bethnal Green Museum,
Cambridge Heath Road,
London, E.2

4⅜"

1⅛"

incised bead

29½"

16⅞"

section
through
tops

Mahogany Chest of Drawers
Serpentine Front About 1760

There is invariably a certain characteristic quality about a serpentine-front chest of drawers. It is obviously much more expensive to make than a flat-front chest, and more so even than the bow-front. This means that in its nature it is fairly costly, and therefore likely to have good work put into it. In the best chests the ends are also shaped, at least partially. If the plan view is examined it will be seen that the end edges of the top follow a somewhat similar shape to that of the front. The chest ends themselves (see section) curve outwards at the front, the remainder being flat. This produces an interesting feature in the canted corners, these often being decorated with applied frets as in the present case. To enable these canted corners to be formed a wide shallow rebate was worked along the front edge and a thicknessing strip of wood glued in. The shape was worked in this. The rebate was desirable as otherwise the applied piece would finish with a feather edge. In extra quality chests the serpentine shape was continued right across to the back. This was necessarily expensive because it meant

thicknessing the ends by another $\frac{7}{8}$ in. or so, quite apart from the extra work involved in working the shape. It was of course necessary to keep the inside flat because the drawers had to run against them.

Drawer fronts are of pine veneered with figured mahogany. Ends are solid mahogany with plain, straight grain. Drawer sides and backs are oak. The top drawer has grooves along the sides a short way down, and was no doubt originally fitted out to hold the usual necessities of the dressing table. This is further borne out by its depth which is greater than that below it. Cocked beads are fitted around all drawers. When a moulding had to be worked around a shaped edge it was clearly impossible to use a moulding plane. Instead the scratch stock was generally used. One occasionally finds exceptions, however, in a moulding decorated with carving in which the actual section was worked by the carver. This is shown by the quite considerable variation found at different positions along the curve. Shaped drawer fronts are usually built up brick fashion.

52

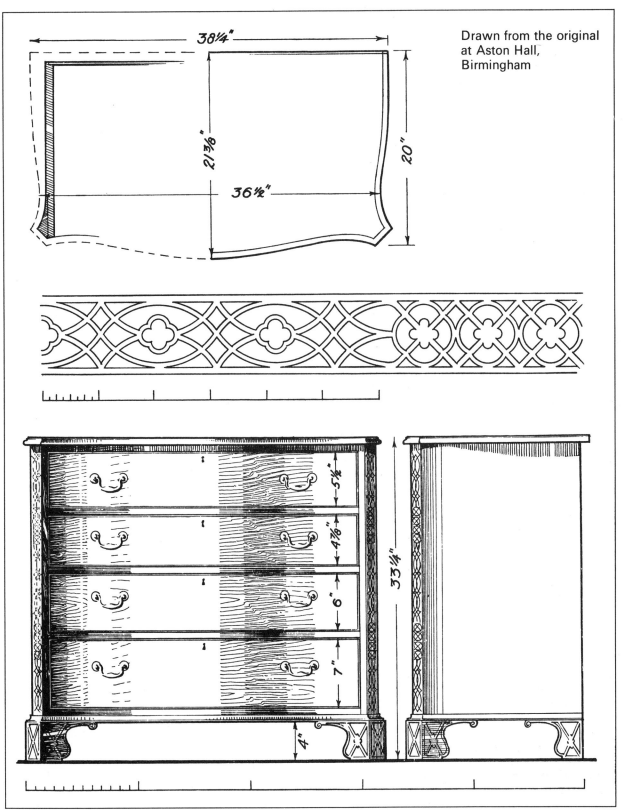

Drawn from the original
at Aston Hall,
Birmingham

38¼"

21⅜"

20"

36½"

5½"

4⅞"

6"

7"

33¼"

4"

Mahogany Dining-side Table About 1760

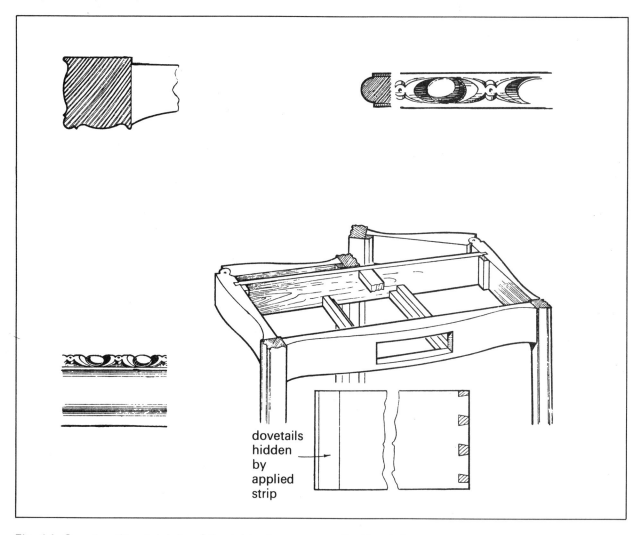

dovetails
hidden
by
applied
strip

Fig. 14. Constructional details of the table shown opposite. Top left
is a section through the leg. The inner corner is chamfered beneath the rail.
The front rail is a solid piece with an opening cut in it to take the drawer.

The table is unusual in the arrangement of the legs. In the closed position the back legs meet at the centre, so that the table has virtually three legs. When opened they swing out to the corners, the top itself folding outwards with card-table hinges so that there are no projecting knuckles on the surface. The table is clearly intended for dining rather than for cards since it shows a polished surface whether in the open or closed position. Wood knuckle hinges

are cut on the side rails and fly rails to enable the legs to pivot, and it will be noted that the length of the side has to be arranged so that the back legs just meet when folded inwards. An interesting feature is in the design of the knuckle joints of the pivoted legs which can move through 90 degrees only. At the inside they are shouldered at 45 degrees each in the usual way, but at the outside, they project beyond the circular line of the knuckle and are

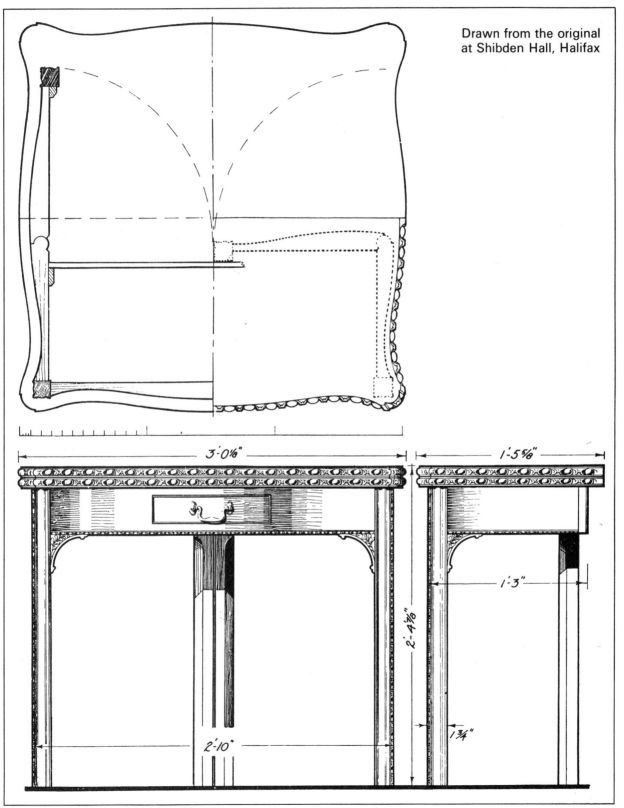

Drawn from the original
at Shibden Hall, Halifax

3'-0⅛"

1'-5⅝"

2'-4⅜"

1'-3"

1¾"

2'-10"

cut square. Thus, when in the open position the joint is entirely concealed except for the plain cross line of the shoulder. The latter also forms a stop which prevents the rail from opening too far.

The whole table is of first quality. The wood is mahogany veneered on mahogany, the rails being built out locally to enable the serpentine shape to be worked. The carving, which follows the conventional pattern of the period, is well and deeply cut. An unusual feature is the provision of solid carved brackets at the juncture of the legs and rails. Where such brackets were fitted they generally took the form of fretted pieces or even simple shaped and carved scrolls, and were decorative rather than constructional. In the present case they may have been a later addition, though there is no sign that the joints have failed.

An examination of the underside of the fixed top reveals a curious and unusual feature. At first glance it appears to be clamped at the ends, but a closer examination reveals that the end edges show end grain. In all probability, therefore, the 'clamps' are simply cross-pieces let in at the underside only—unless pieces of cross-grain stuff have been tongued on outside the clamps. The upper side only of this fixed top is veneered, the veneer being thick—almost an overlay.

Both sides of the hinged top are veneered. This was probably considered necessary because, whereas the fixed top is fixed rigidly to the framework, the hinged one is entirely self-supporting.

Mahogany Chair of the Chippendale Period

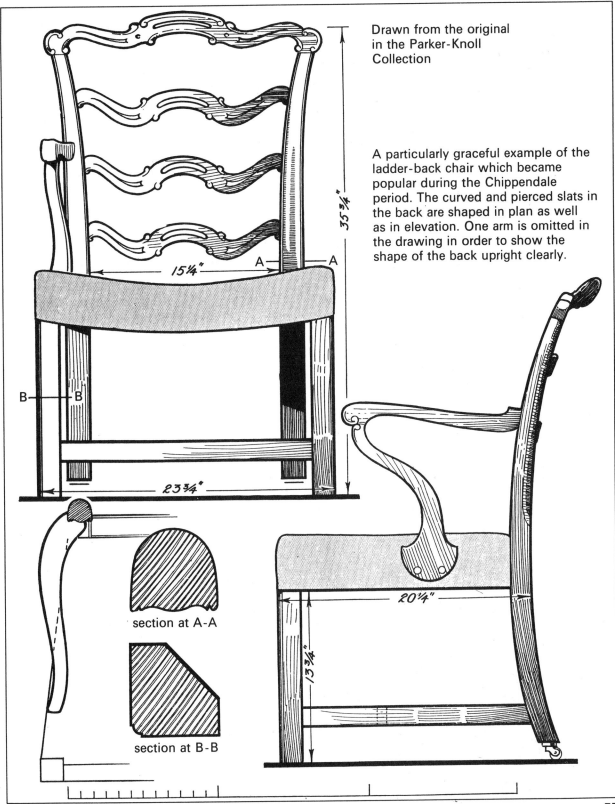

Drawn from the original
in the Parker-Knoll
Collection

A particularly graceful example of the
ladder-back chair which became
popular during the Chippendale
period. The curved and pierced slats in
the back are shaped in plan as well
as in elevation. One arm is omitted in
the drawing in order to show the
shape of the back upright clearly.

35¾"

15¼"

23¾"

20¼"

13¾"

A — A

B — B

section at A-A

section at B-B

Grandfather Clock Mid 18th century

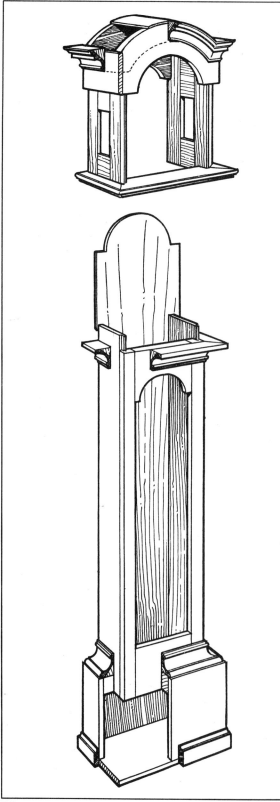

Fig. 15. Probable construction of the clockcase. The front of the waist is made up as a frame and the ends are tongued to it.

This is a particularly well-proportioned clockcase, and is free from the overdone detail and pompous proportions that spoil many cases of the period. The hood is made to draw forwards, and separates from the waist as shown by the dotted line in the hood-waist mould section. In the frieze is a pierced metal overlay with red plush background showing through. On the dial appears the maker's name, *Walter Partridge, London.*

Construction details are given in Fig. 15. The waist consists of a front framework fixed to the ends with a tongued joint. Both project downwards a few inches into the sur-base, thicknessing pieces are added, and the sur-base panels glued on over these. A bottom is fixed, and the plinth mitred round. At the top the front frame finishes level with the waist portion of the hood-waist moulding. The ends, however, stand up beyond to give support to the movement platform. They also enable slips to be applied round which the moulding of the hood can engage. This allows the whole hood to draw forward without danger of its toppling outwards. In most grandfather clock cases the waist door is clamped, though not invariably. The odd thing is that in many such doors there is no tongued-and-grooved joint as one might expect. Quite frequently the clamps were merely butted and glued. Of course, the veneer, in passing across the whole surface, served to strengthen the parts, but it seems a rather odd arrangement, and was a method apparently confined to clockcase makers. It is clear too that there was a special branch of the trade that confined itself to case making as distinct from furniture making. It often shows in the sections of mouldings which were usually of different patterns from those used by cabinet makers. The hood is built up as shown. Note that there is an inner framing piece behind the door, so that the dial still looks neat when the door is opened. The curved moulding, being circular, would be turned. This would provide enough for two clocks, and it is an intriguing thought that somewhere or other there is probably another case (if it has survived) on which the rest of the moulding was used. A point to note is that it is necessary to cut a curved mitre at the intersection of the curved and straight portions.

21½"

20¾"

STRIKE
SILENT

12"

65½"

13⅞"

13½"

18"

Drawn from the original
standing in Hampton
Court Palace

7"

9"

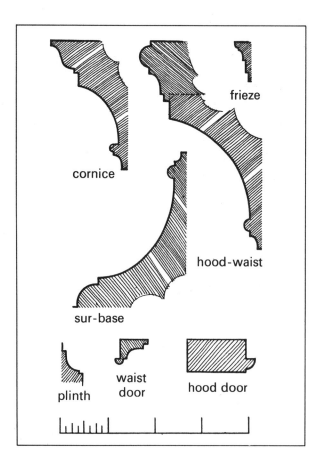

cornice

frieze

hood-waist

sur-base

plinth

waist door

hood door

The same thing applies to the moulding on the waist door, though here the moulding is comparatively narrow and the difference would not be noticeable. If a straight mitre were cut it would be necessary for the section of the straight part to vary from that of the curved portion.

For the dial door acorn hinges are used, the knuckles being set well forward (about $\frac{5}{16}$ in.) clear of the door face. Otherwise there are complications in the hinging. In any case the top of the door has to be cut away at the back internal corner of the hinging side to enable it to clear the corner of the frieze mould as the door opens.

Mahogany Book Shelves Late 18th century

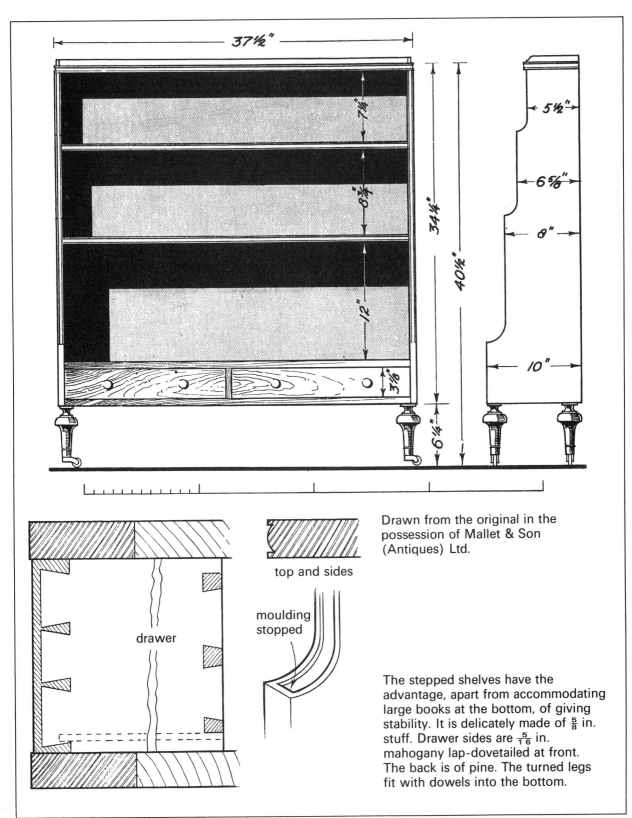

Drawn from the original in the possession of Mallet & Son (Antiques) Ltd.

top and sides

drawer

moulding stopped

The stepped shelves have the advantage, apart from accommodating large books at the bottom, of giving stability. It is delicately made of $\frac{5}{8}$ in. stuff. Drawer sides are $\frac{5}{16}$ in. mahogany lap-dovetailed at front. The back is of pine. The turned legs fit with dowels into the bottom.

Mahogany Bookcase Late 18th century

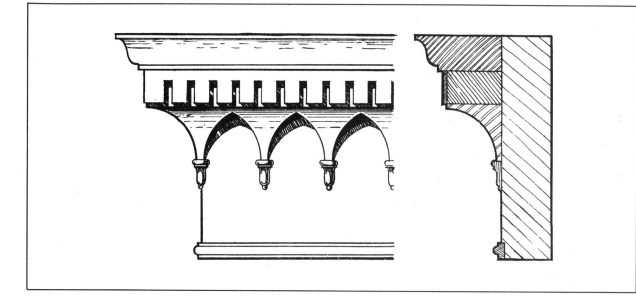

Fig. 16. Enlarged detail of cornice moulding.
Commonly cornice mouldings were made up
with a backing of softwood, the joint running up
at an angle as that on page 47. In fact Sheraton
in one of his books gives in detail the method of
working such a moulding. In the present case
the large hollow member is fretted and would
need to show solid wood throughout.

This was a popular type of bookcase during the
second half of the eighteenth century. The
upper portion invariably was a bookcase with
barred doors and the lower part a cupboard.
Frequently the cupboard was considerably
deeper than the bookcase.

The moulding of the glazing is a simple $\frac{3}{8}$-in.
astragal fitted over $\frac{1}{8}$-in. bars. The fretted cornice
is particularly effective. As shown in Fig. 16
the fretted member would be made separately
and glued on after polishing, the polish being
scraped away locally. Small split turnings form
the pendants. The wood for these would be in
two thicknesses glued together with paper in
62

the joint. After turning the joint is easily split
open. Frequently such pendants were in ivory.
Flush panels are fitted to the lower doors. They
are grooved into the framework and the astragal
moulding applied over the joints.

The main carcase is in two parts, each being
lap-dovetailed together. In the best way both
cornice and plinth would be made as complete
separate items and would be screwed in
position or held with wood blocks.

Drawn from the original in the possession
of M. Harris & Sons

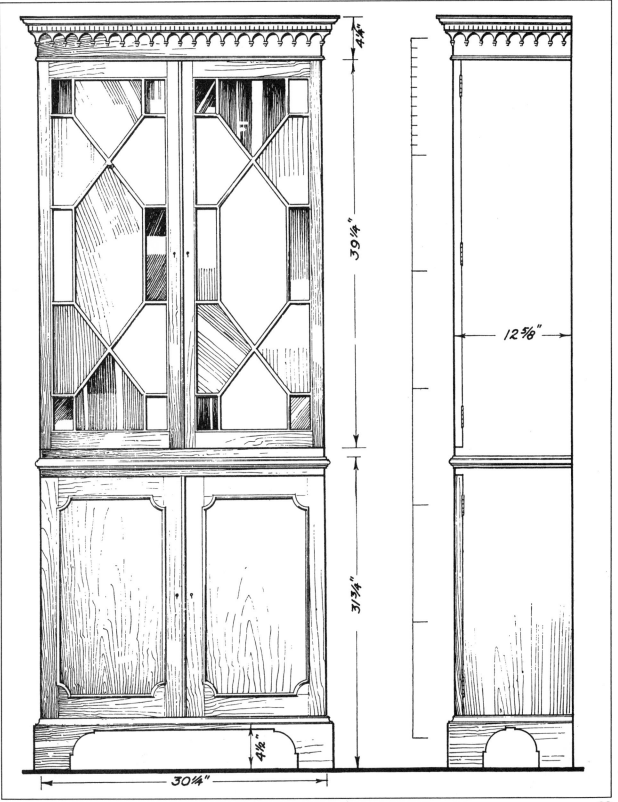

4¼"

39¼"

12⅝"

31¾"

4½"

30¼"

Mahogany Toilet Mirror Late 18th century

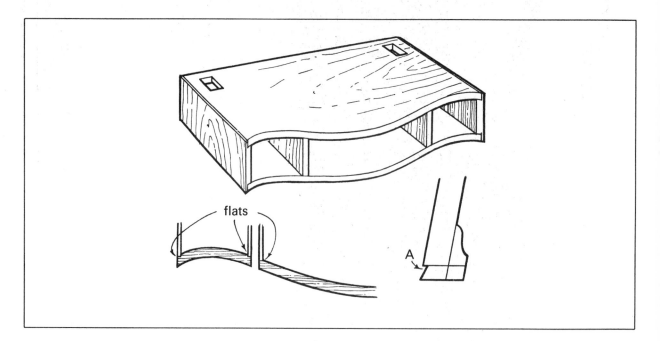

Fig. 17. Details of main box and drawers.
Drawers are dovetailed. (A) shows joint at
foot of standard.

These were popular items towards the end of the
eighteenth century. Both oval and shield-shape,
and occasionally rectangular, mirrors were used.
The better kinds had bow- or serpentine-shaped
fronts as here, cheaper ones being flat. The
present example has satinwood inlay lines
around the drawers, and a fruitwood cross-
banding around the top. An interesting note is
that the drawer dovetails have an extremely
flat angle, being only a degree or two from the
parallel. Drawer fronts are $\frac{7}{16}$ in. thick and sides
and backs (oak) $\frac{1}{8}$ in. The mirror is pivoted a

trifle above centre so that it tends to keep
position even when the fixing nuts are not
tightened.
The main box has a simple lapped joint, the
parts being glued and pinned. Thick saw-cut
veneer conceals the joints. The tenon of the
standard is hooked at the point as at A, Fig. 17.
The back corner, to prevent any tendency for
it to be forced back, is often rounded. This
should be borne in mind when it is necessary to
repair. The standard should be pulled forward to
get it out, not pulled straight up.

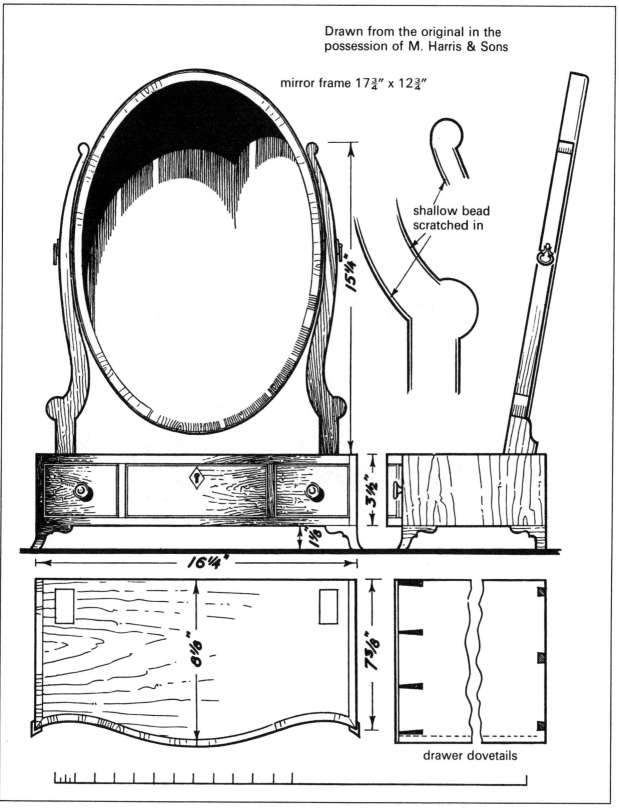

Drawn from the original in the
possession of M. Harris & Sons

mirror frame 17¾" x 12¾"

shallow bead
scratched in

15¼"

3½"

1⅛"

16¼"

8⅙"

7⅝"

drawer dovetails

Mahogany Table About 1780

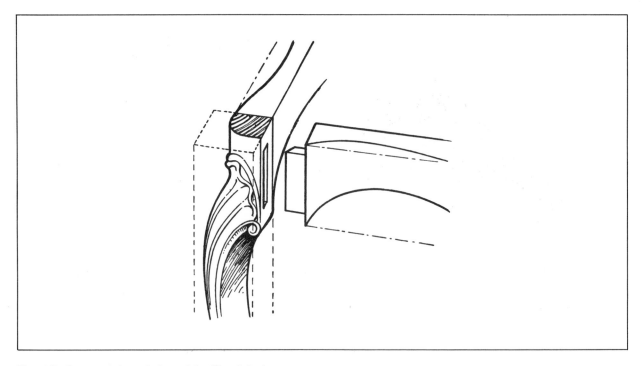

Fig. 18. Corner joint of the table. The jointing would have been completed before the shaping was worked. Allowance for the curve would have been made when fixing the mortise position.

The serpentine-shaping was a popular feature in small tables towards the end of the eighteenth century. In cheaper work the top only was shaped, the framework remaining rectangular. Here, however, the veneered frame follows the line of the top. The cabriole legs are suggestive of French influence.

In making the rails the usual plan is to cut them straight and square and tenon them. The plan shape is worked (a bandsaw offers the simplest and best method), the surface veneered, and finally the lower edge shaped. If preferred the latter could be completed before veneering. The dotted lines in Fig. 18 show the square of timber required to enable the cabriole legs to be worked.

An unusual feature is that the inlay around the the top stands proud of the surface. The groove for this would be worked first and the inlay fitted in dry. It is then removed and the top cleaned up. After gluing the whole is then cleaned up. The three pieces would not be put together beforehand as a banding because separate inlays are able to negotiate the curve more easily.

Drawn from the original in the Georgian House, City Art Gallery, Bristol

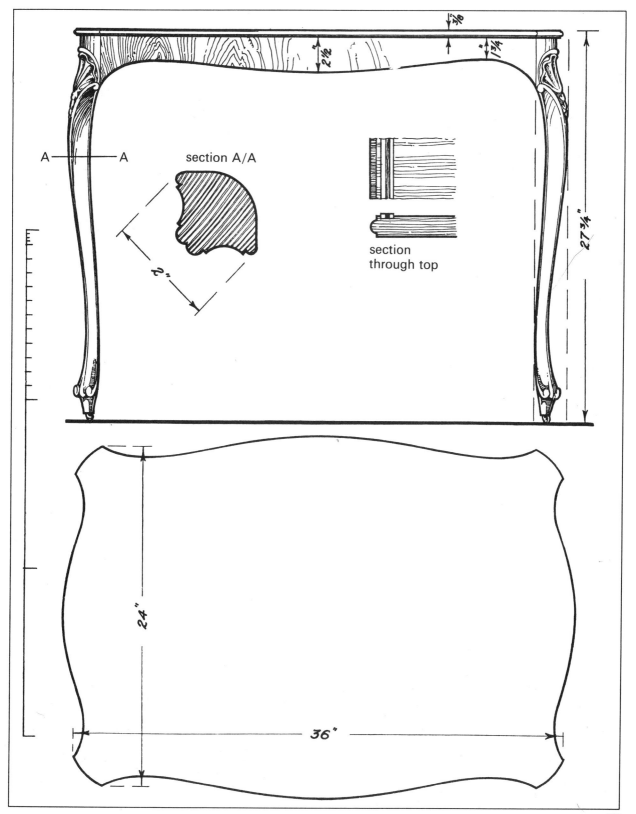

section A/A

2"

section
through top

⅜"

2½"

1¾"

27¾"

A —— A

24"

36"

Mahogany Dining Table Late 18th century

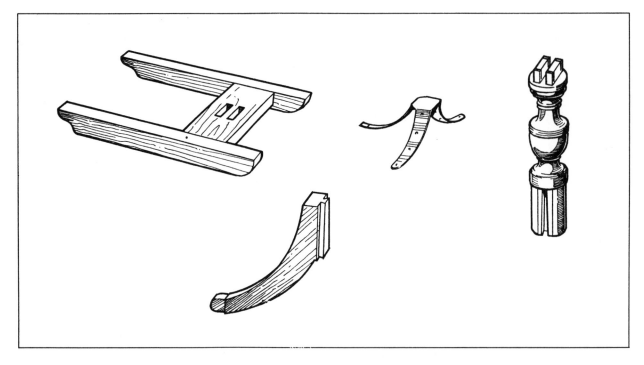

Fig. 19. Construction of dining table

The tripod table was used extensively towards the end of the eighteenth century and in the early part of the nineteenth century. As a rule the legs were spaced evenly at 120 degrees. The present example is unusual in that the two side legs diverge from a straight line only slightly. Fig. 19 shows how the legs are taper slot-dovetailed to the centre pillar. A metal plate screwed beneath serves to bind all three together. At the top the pillar is through-tenoned into a cross-piece and wedged. The cross-piece in turn is tenoned to bearers. The leaf has dowels or short tongues to engage with the top, and is kept in position by metal locking devices (see dotted lines in plan view). Many of these tables had slides fitting in boxed sleeves beneath the main top to give the leaf additional support.

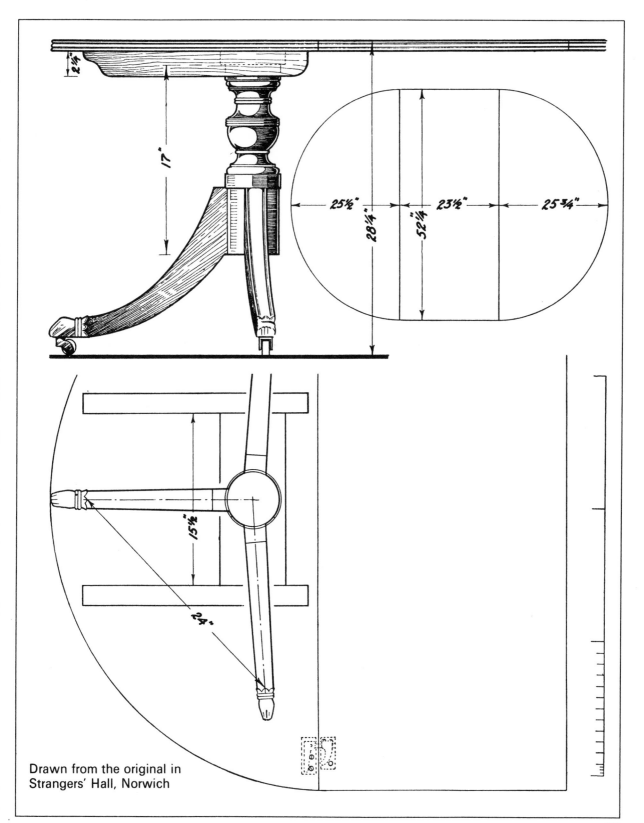

2¼"

17"

25½"   23½"   25¾"

28¼"

52¼"

15½"

24"

Drawn from the original in
Strangers' Hall, Norwich

Mahogany Corner Cupboard 18th century

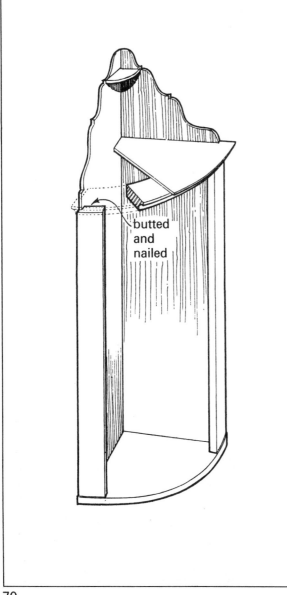

butted
and
nailed

Fig. 20. Construction of corner cupboard. Two $\frac{1}{4}$-in. shelves are fitted inside, these resting upon fillets glued and nailed to the backs.

This attractive cupboard is in curl mahogany veneered on oak. The bow doors are jointed together cooper fashion and veneered on the outside only. Backs (which continue up to form the top shaping) and shelves are in oak. Construction is surprisingly simple. At the top is a shaped and moulded rail glued and nailed down on to the pilasters. A similar idea is followed at the bottom, but the latter extends right to the corner instead of being just a rail. The pilasters are merely butted. Despite this simplicity the cupboard is as sound today as when it was made. Cabinet makers knew the value of close-fitting joints, and understood how to use animal glue effectively.
The oak backs continue upwards, shaped as shown, and have the small curved shelf contained between them. Two shelves are fitted inside the cupboard. The decorative hinges are in brass. A simple lock is fitted, this being screwed on inside without being let in.
As the doors are veneered on the outside only one might have expected them to have pulled flat, but there is no sign of this. They follow the line of the top and bottom closely. One wonders whether the craftsman worked the other way round, making the doors first, and cutting the shape of the top and bottom to align with the doors. There has been no attempt to clean up the inside surfaces of the doors with accuracy. They do in fact show plane marks roughly in line with the length of the doors, a round plane of slightly quicker curvature than that of the door having been used.

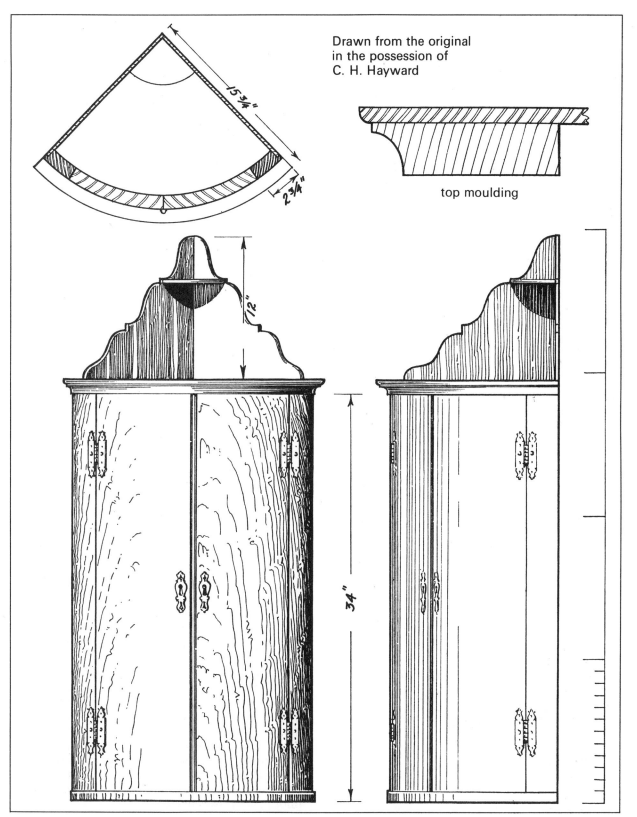

Drawn from the original
in the possession of
C. H. Hayward

15 3/4"

2 3/4"

top moulding

12"

34"

Mahogany Pembroke Table Second half 18th century

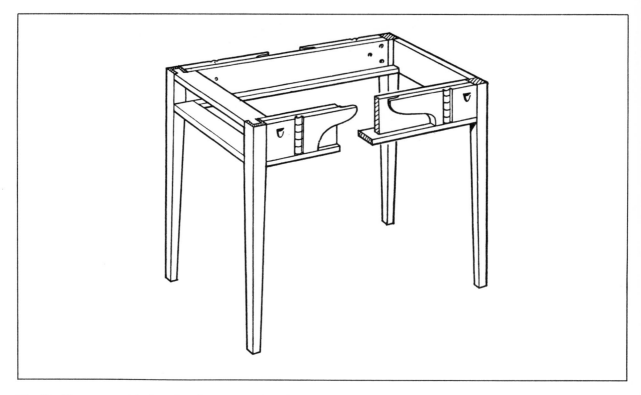

Fig. 21. Top removed showing frame construction

This is typical of a form of table which became popular during the second half of the eighteenth century. Some had tops of rectangular form, others had the corners rounded as in the present example, a third type was of a rather wide elliptical shape, and yet another kind had serpentine outline. The leaves were invariably supported by shaped brackets pivoted on knuckle joints. Mostly the tables were inlaid with bandings and strings.

The taper of the legs is planed on the inner surfaces only. All rails are tenoned to the legs except the top drawer rail which is lap-dovetailed. Note that the long rails stand in to enable the brackets and their stub-rails to fit in flush with the legs. Construction varies in different tables, but in many the stub-rails were tenoned into the legs, and a thinner joining rail butted between the legs and screwed and glued to the sub-rails. The advantage of this method is that the tenons are nearer the outer surfaces of the legs and can thus be of maximum length.

72

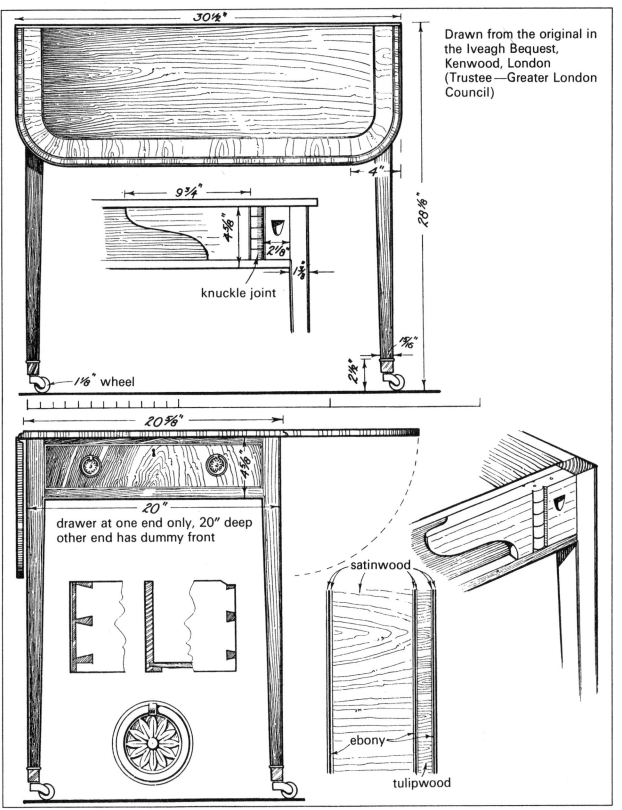

30½"

Drawn from the original in
the Iveagh Bequest,
Kenwood, London
(Trustee—Greater London
Council)

4"

9¾"

4⅝"

2⅛"

1⅜"

knuckle joint

28⅛"

15⁄16"

2½"

1⅛" wheel

20⅝"

4⅝"

20"

drawer at one end only, 20" deep
other end has dummy front

satinwood

ebony

tulipwood

73

Mahogany Card Table Second half 18th century

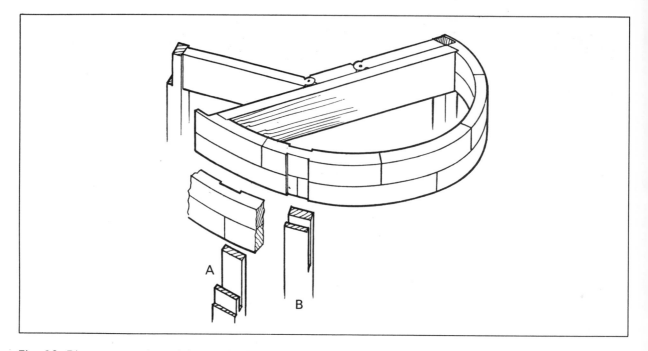

Fig. 22. Rim construction of the card table

The semicircular rim of the table is veneered with mahogany on a softwood groundwork. The latter is built up brick fashion with two layers. The vertical joints are butted and are staggered so that the layers support each other. A more usual form of construction is to have about four thicknesses rather than two. The back rail is lap-dovetailed into the ends which are notched and cut back to allow the back legs to fit in. A form of bridle joint is used for the two front legs and might be either as at A or B, Fig. 22. The back legs are joined to the fly rails with the usual mortise and tenon. A refinement in the fly rails is the rounded groove at the top edges to hold the baize which is glued in,

avoiding any tendency for the edges to work up. The boxwood line around the edge of the top protects the edge of the veneer.
The legs are moulded, the scratch stock being used for the purpose. Since they are tapered, only one half of the contour is worked at a time, the remaining half being finished with the same tool worked from the other face. It will be realised that the outer beads are the same width all the way down. The variation in section due to the taper takes place in the large centre member only. This process necessarily leaves an unworked flat in the middle which is finished by passing a plane along the corners and finishing with glasspaper wrapped around a shaped block.

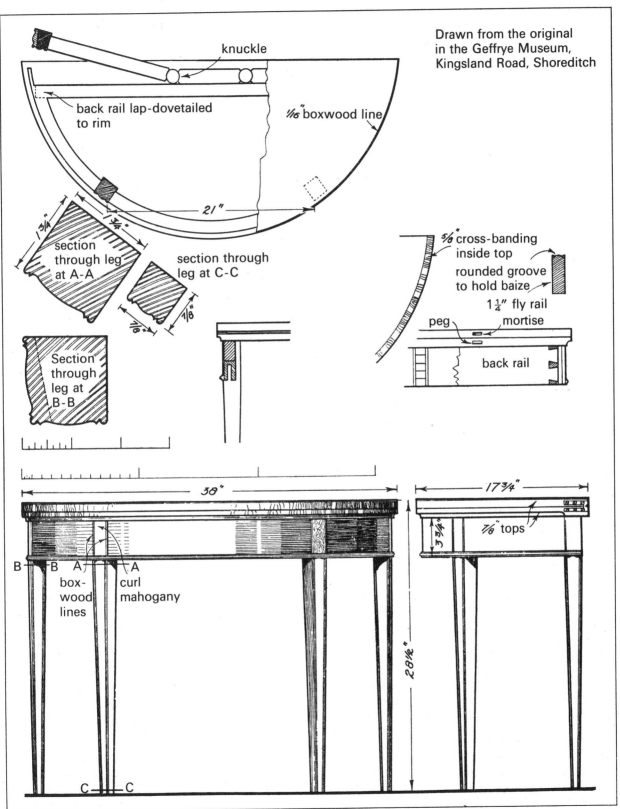

knuckle

back rail lap-dovetailed to rim

$\frac{1}{16}$" boxwood line

Drawn from the original in the Geffrye Museum, Kingsland Road, Shoreditch

$\frac{3}{4}$"

$1\frac{3}{4}$"

section through leg at A-A

section through leg at C-C

$\frac{7}{8}$

$\frac{1}{16}$"

Section through leg at B-B

21"

$\frac{5}{16}$" cross-banding inside top

rounded groove to hold baize

$1\frac{1}{4}$" fly rail mortise

peg

back rail

38"

$17\frac{3}{4}$"

$3\frac{3}{4}$"

$\frac{7}{8}$" tops

$28\frac{1}{2}$"

B — B   A — A

box-wood lines

curl mahogany

C — C

Mahogany Nest of Tables   Late 18th century

These are extremely delicately made. The squares from which the turnings are made finish $\frac{7}{8}$ in. only. In all probability a face plate was used in place of the normal centre, this having a block of wood screwed to it with a square recess in it to receive the wood. This would automatically centre the wood. All twelve legs are a very close match, and the turning would require considerable skill for they would be extremely liable to whip, being so thin and long.

The taper is slight—less than $\frac{1}{4}$ in. over the whole length. No doubt a steady was used on the lathe, and would have been of the type still used by some Wycombe turners. It consists of a sort of open-fronted box which can be fixed in any position along the lathe bed. Pivoted to it is a nearly vertical piece of wood notched to bear against the turning. A wedge at the back drops by its own weight and automatically keeps the pivoted piece up to the turning. The latter is thus supported at the back and it is in fact possible to turn right opposite the steady, the pivoted piece being kept up to the work by the wedge dropping as the diameter is reduced.

At top and bottom the legs are tenoned into the cross members and feet. The last named are tapered towards the bottom, and rebates are worked in the cross members of the two larger tables so that they slide one within the other. A bead is planted round the edges of all the tops, this fitting in a rebate as shown by the enlarged section. In all probability the tops are screwed to the cross-members, the heads being recessed and the holes plugged. The surface would then have been veneered afterwards.

It will be realised that although each smaller table is a fairly close fit beneath the next larger one, there must be some clearance. This might be about $\frac{1}{16}$ in. above the beads surrounding the tops.

At the bottom the legs are jointed by the curved stretchers which are cut in the solid and glued and pinned into sloping notches cut in the back edges of the legs. They would certainly be stronger if laminated and bent. Fixing, too, would be stronger if small brass screws were used rather than pins, though glue would still be needed.

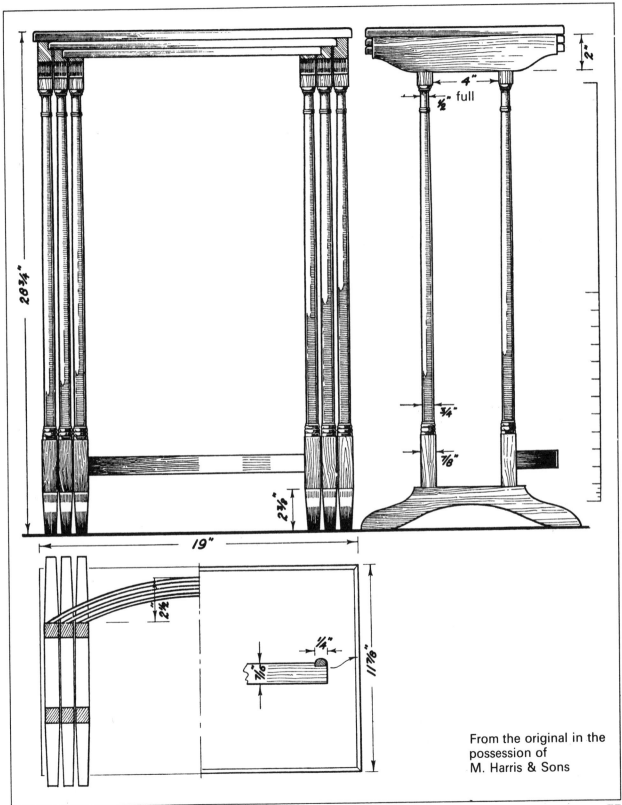

28¾"

2"

4"

½" full

¾"

⅞"

2⅝"

19"

2½"

11⅝"

¼"

9/16"

From the original in the
possession of
M. Harris & Sons

Mahogany Serpentine-front Sideboard
Late 18th century

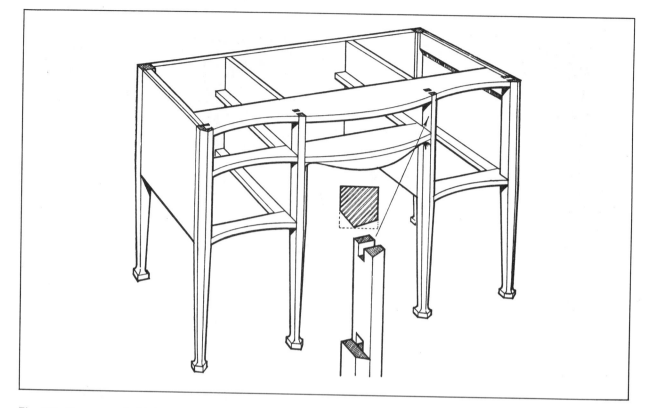

Fig. 23. Carcase of sideboard with drawers removed. The enlarged drawing shows how middle legs are cut away at top, this forming square surfaces against which the middle drawer can run.

The piece shown opposite is of special interest in that it embodies a feature seldom found in serpentine-front sideboards; the legs follow the curve of the front. In most sideboards of the type the legs are rectangular in section and are set square with the ends and back, and this necessarily involves a break in the curved line. In the present case the section of the legs enables the curve to be continuous (note the enlarged section which gives the effect of the legs being set at an angle). This makes the construction more difficult and expensive, but adds tremendously to the appearance.

Fig. 23 shows how the main carcase is made. With the exception of the two back ones, none

of the legs is square. The dotted lines in the plan view (page 79) make this clear. The two outer front legs are made as in the enlarged section (A-A) on the same page. Note that back, outer, and inner faces are square with each other, this simplifying the joints, and enabling the drawers to run against square faces. At the front the legs are planed so that they align with the canted corner and also follow the curve of the front. Turning to the inner legs, these also are set square to simplify the joints. The front is planed to follow the plan shaping, and the corner facing the middle is taken off so that it balances the outer legs. This makes a complication in that at the top there would not be a square surface for

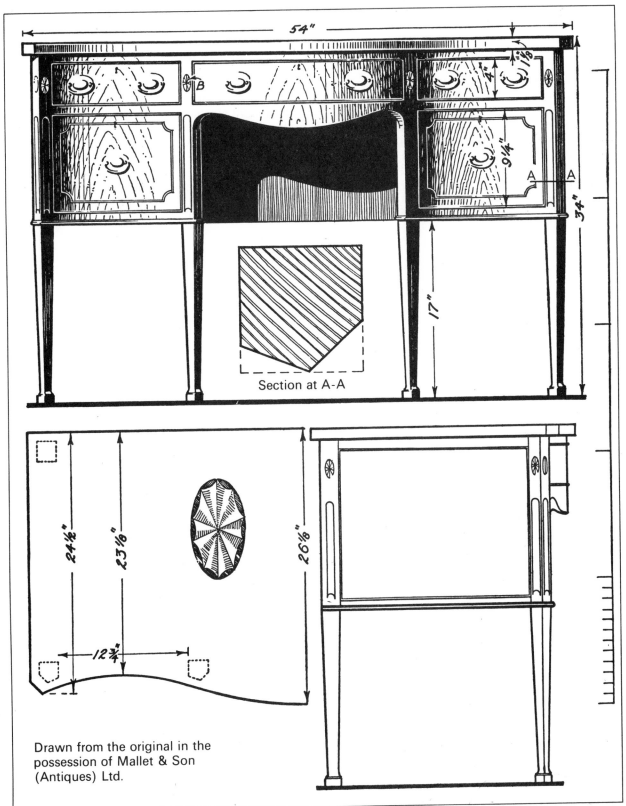

Section at A-A

Drawn from the original in the
possession of Mallet & Son
(Antiques) Ltd.

the drawer to run against. Fig. 23 shows how by cutting back the leg at the top the square surface can be obtained. Note that the notch includes the drawer rail which fits into the mortise as shown. The shaping of the rail is secured by building up the thickness and bow-sawing to shape. The front would be veneered afterwards.

All the rails are tenoned in except the top front one which is lap-dovetailed at the ends, and has a form of bridle joint to hold the inner legs. The back, which is a solid piece of $\frac{7}{8}$ in. stuff, is also tenoned in.

The cabinet work is of a very high standard, as is shown by the delicate satinwood inlay, the thin cocked beads, and the fine finish. At the right-hand side the 'two' drawers open as one, so forming a deep cellaret drawer, and the drawer sides have the characteristic shaped notches cut into the top edges, the purpose of which is to enable the metal liner to be withdrawn easily. Both serpentine-front and bow-front sideboards were popular towards the end of the eighteenth century.

Quite frequently the space between the inner legs contained a cupboard which could be slid forward on runners. It was usually enclosed by a tambour, this following the general curve of the sideboard. Often the tambour was of alternate strips of mahogany and satinwood.

Adjustable Candle Stand Mid 18th century

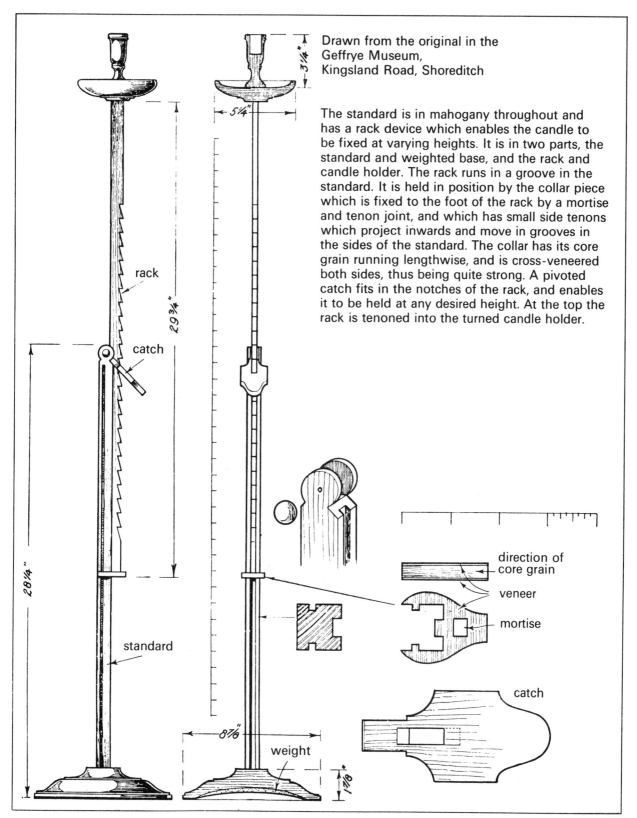

Drawn from the original in the
Geffrye Museum,
Kingsland Road, Shoreditch

The standard is in mahogany throughout and
has a rack device which enables the candle to
be fixed at varying heights. It is in two parts, the
standard and weighted base, and the rack and
candle holder. The rack runs in a groove in the
standard. It is held in position by the collar piece
which is fixed to the foot of the rack by a mortise
and tenon joint, and which has small side tenons
which project inwards and move in grooves in
the sides of the standard. The collar has its core
grain running lengthwise, and is cross-veneered
both sides, thus being quite strong. A pivoted
catch fits in the notches of the rack, and enables
it to be held at any desired height. At the top the
rack is tenoned into the turned candle holder.

rack

catch

29¾"

28¼"

standard

5¼"

3¼"

6⅞"

1⅛"

weight

direction of
core grain

veneer

mortise

catch

Mahogany Writing Table Late 18th century

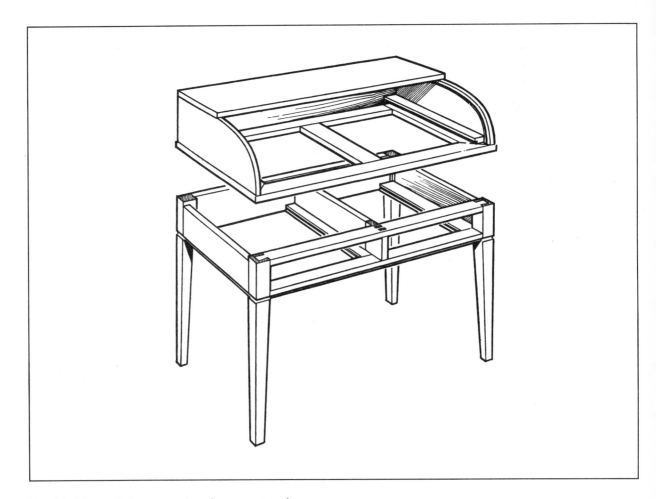

Fig. 24. View of the parts showing construction.
It is made in two separate parts, stand and upper
carcase. The two are put together with screws.

Furniture associated with the Sheraton period
was invariably of neat, delicate form, and was
frequently fitted with mechanical movements
and devices. In the present example the writing
space is enclosed by a tambour, and the writing
top is made to slide forward when in use. In
addition the centre portion of the writing top is
hinged so that it can be raised and used as a
reading stand, being supported by a simple rack
device. At each side are pull-out slides to hold
papers, etc. The drawer handles are of especially
fine quality, consisting of a brass casing or
edging with decorative wood centre. Note that
the entire taper of the legs is planed from the
inside.
A piece of this kind would be made in two main
sections, the main lower table consisting of the

legs and their rails, and the writing top, ends,
and tambour. Taking the former, the end rails
are tenoned into the legs, and are set down at
the top to leave space for the slides which pull
out. Back and lower front rail are also tenoned in,
but the top front rail is dovetailed.
The base of the upper portion consists of a
framework level with the lower reeded moulding
(B). The latter in fact is mitred round it. This
frame is dowelled and screwed to the ends (A),
and the top (B) probably positioned with stub-
dowels and pocket screwed. The writing top is a
separate item made up as a frame and slides
forward. It has tongues at the sides which
engage with grooves worked in fixed pieces
running from front to back in the lower internal
corners of the upper portion. At (D) is given the

Drawn from the original in the possession of the
Society for the Protection of Ancient Buildings

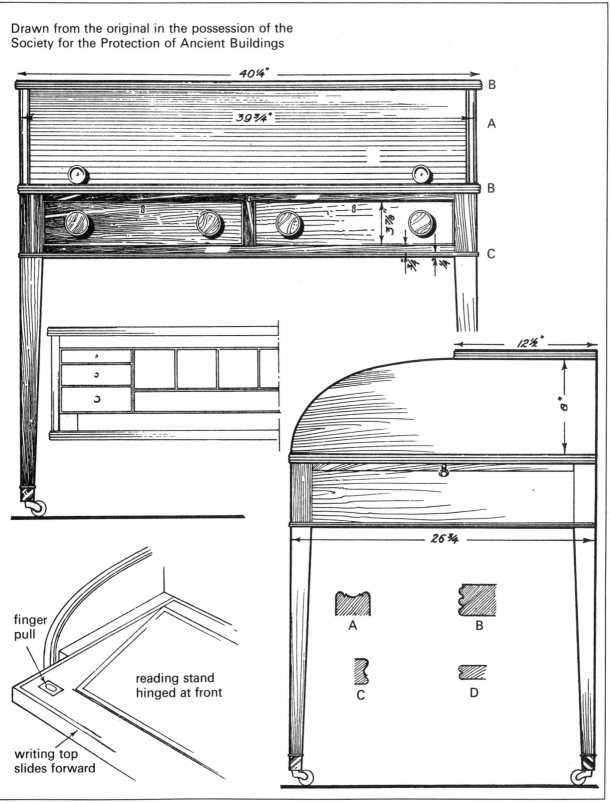

finger
pull

reading stand
hinged at front

writing top
slides forward

tambour section. The moulded strips are glued down on to canvas, and run in curved grooves worked around the edges of the ends.

A tambour of this kind can bend in one direction only. It clearly had to be fed in after the main carcase had been assembled, and it was often necessary to continue its groove to run out at either back or bottom. After finally fitting and polishing the tambour the run-out grooves would be filled in, the tambour thus bypassing them. In the present case it could be fed in at the rear, the back being added later. After filling in the run-out groove the tambour would pass around a curved groove near the back and continue towards the bottom.

As these tambour slats are fairly wide they would be made as separate pieces and the canvas glued to them. In the case of narrow slats of bead section quite often they were made of two beads to a slat. One advantage of a bead section is that it will pass around a curve of reverse section providing the curve is not too acute. The bottom slat which holds the lock is usually wider than the others.

Child's High Chair About 1820

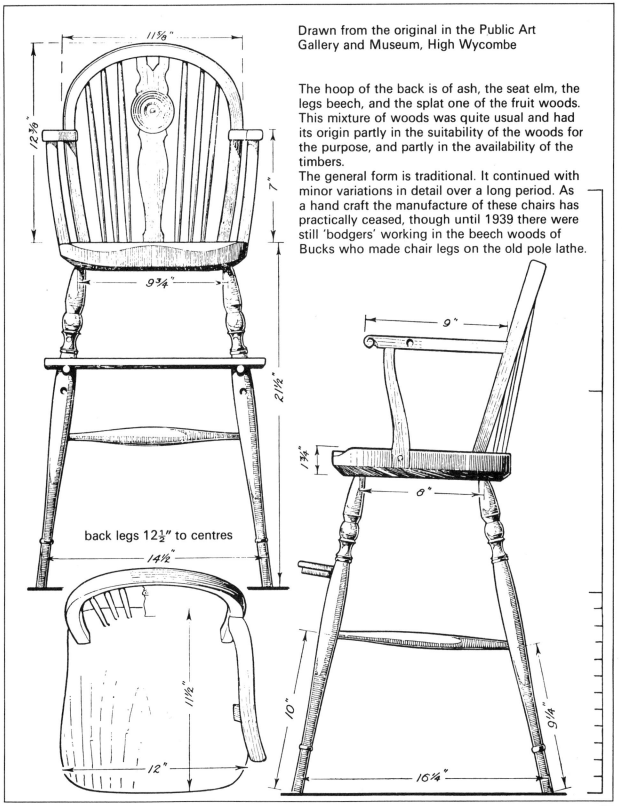

Drawn from the original in the Public Art
Gallery and Museum, High Wycombe

The hoop of the back is of ash, the seat elm, the
legs beech, and the splat one of the fruit woods.
This mixture of woods was quite usual and had
its origin partly in the suitability of the woods for
the purpose, and partly in the availability of the
timbers.
The general form is traditional. It continued with
minor variations in detail over a long period. As
a hand craft the manufacture of these chairs has
practically ceased, though until 1939 there were
still 'bodgers' working in the beech woods of
Bucks who made chair legs on the old pole lathe.

11⅝"

12⅜"

7"

9¾"

21½"

back legs 12½" to centres

14½"

11½"

12"

9"

1¾"

8"

10"

9¼"

16¼"

Mahogany Bureau Bookcase Regency period

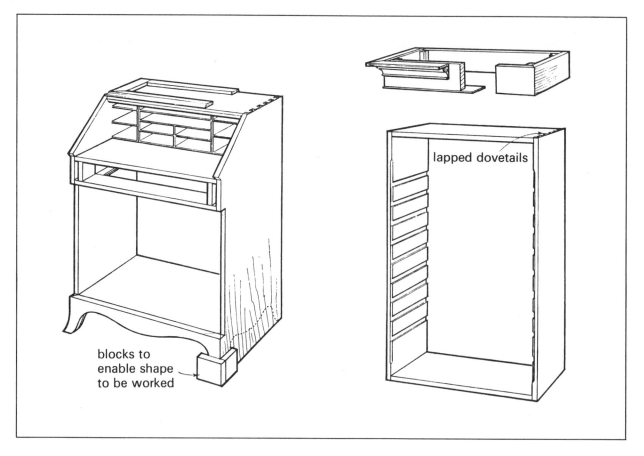

blocks to enable shape to be worked

lapped dovetails

Fig. 25 Construction of the two carcases, and details of cornice. Note the way that the shaped plinth is built up with blocks to enable the curved surface to be worked. After shaping and cleaning up the whole is veneered.

Drawn from the original in the possession of M. Harris & Sons

There are two unusual features about the proportions of this piece, one being the height of the writing top ($32\frac{1}{2}$ in.) this being $2\frac{1}{2}$ in. higher than normal. The other is the depth of the bookcase, this being quite unnecessary for average books. Probably there was a special reason for both features. Cornice and frieze are made as a separate item, and are held in position by the usual corner blocks. An interesting and unusual detail is the section of the cornice. It is of a most delicate and refined contour, and is enriched with shallow dentils hollowed at the underside. In the frieze is an applied brass decoration half-round in section with acanthus and husk detail and scrolled ends.

The traceried doors have a neat three-bead moulding fitting over the bars. The glass is puttied in.
Most bureaus of this type were provided throughout with drawers. In the present case there is a cupboard with single shelf beneath the drawer, this being enclosed by flush doors with cross-banded edges and an inlaid string.
Beneath the fall is a simple stationery nest with drawers and pigeon holes.
Lower carcase construction is given in Fig. 25. Lapped dovetails are used at both top and bottom, the former being concealed by the flat moulding planted on top. The cutting away of the ends to receive the doors enables the last

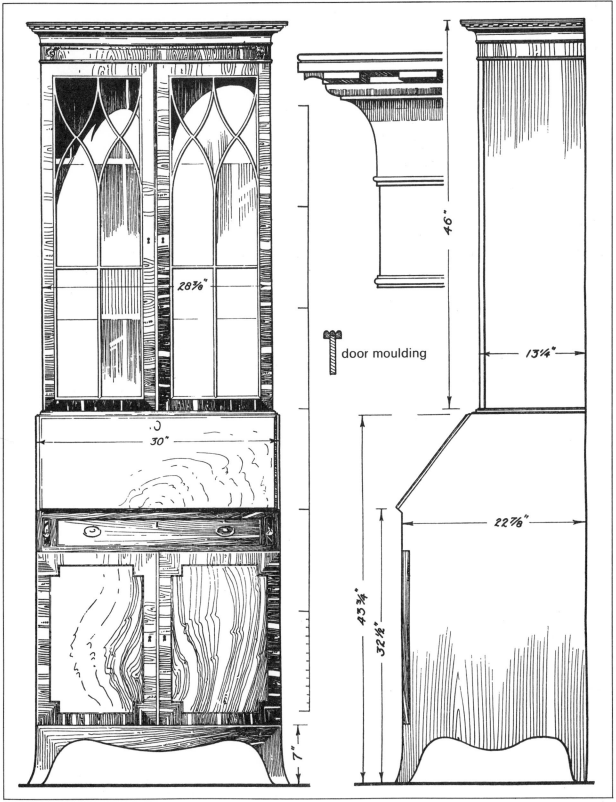

28⅜"

door moulding

46"

13¼"

30"

22⅞"

43¾"

32½"

7"

named to fit across the entire width. This looks more attractive than if they were flanked by the ends. The shaped feet are built up. The ends run right down, and the front corners are mitred to receive the front piece. The latter could be shaped either before or after fixing. When the glue has set a shallow rebate (about $\frac{1}{8}$ in.) is worked around. This is to enable thicknessing pieces to be planted on. Unless this rebate were formed the thicknessing pieces or blocks would end in a feather edge after shaping. Glue blocks are rubbed in all internal angles. The parts are cut to shape and finished with spokeshave and rasp. Veneering follows. There is no difficulty in putting the veneer down with the hammer. As in all such cases, the bottom edges are all well chamfered so that there is no tendency for the veneer to be torn off if the bureau is pulled across the floor.

Doors are flush, and consist of a framework with flush panel. These have a rather unusual construction in that the panels apparently fit in rebates and are glued in. The veneer is taken right over frame and panel. Some well-seasoned stuff must have been used, for there is no sign of any movement.

Upper carcase construction is fairly obvious as shown in Fig. 25. Top and bottom are lap-dovetailed, and the ends are grooved across the inside to receive the shelves. Doors are veneered on the face, and the veneer cut away locally at the inner edges to receive the triple bead. The bars of the tracery are $\frac{1}{8}$ in. thick and are cut to shape in the solid at the curves. It would be stronger to laminate and bend three or four thicknesses of saw-cut veneer. The mouldings fit over the bars, and are worked in the solid wood with the scratch stock.

Door and Framework Construction

Fig. w. Oak framed and panelled door of the mid-seventeenth century with moulded framework, recessed panels, and carving. The effect is obtained by the varying levels of the surfaces and the shadows thrown by them.

Fig. x. Framed door of about 1700 with recessed panel (C), or flush panel (D). The whole is veneered in walnut. The chief decorative effect is obtained by the cross-grained veneer of the framework and the figured and halved panel.

Fig. y. Flush door of the early eighteenth century in walnut veneered over oak in which the effect is produced entirely by the colour and rich grain of the quartering and cross-banding.

Fig. z. Solid mahogany framed door of about 1730–40, a partial reversion to the earlier type, probably owing to the relatively subdued and dark grain of Cuban mahogany. The panel is fielded, and the effect obtained by the shadows formed by the varying levels.

These illustrations are included to show how the introduction of veneering in this country during the seventeenth century fundamentally altered construction. In the oak door in Fig. w the effect is obtained by the variations in level of the different surfaces, the undulating mouldings, the carving, and the shadows and highlights caused by these. In veneered work it is by the grain of the wood and its decorative character and arrangement that the effect is obtained. Thus in Fig. x, although the framework is retained, the rich grain of the halved panel and the cross-grain largely produces the effect. The alternative of a recessed panel is given at (C) and a flush effect at (D). Later the tendency was towards a flush effect as in Fig. y in which appearance is due wholly to grain arrangement In the first half of the eighteenth century Cuban mahogany began to supersede walnut as a furniture wood, and the grain of this, though usually rich, was not so marked as in walnut and was in any case dark. Consequently there was a partial return to the earlier construction of panelled frames as in Fig. z, though it was of a more refined character. A flush door made purely in dark Cuban mahogany would scarcely show the details.

Later in the century the lighter Honduras mahogany was frequently used, and frames were again frequently flush with the decorative effect obtained by inlay lines and bandings, and often with halved and quartered grain in the veneer.

Furniture Through the Ages

The following plates are given, partly for their interest in showing the evolution of design, and partly to enable readers to see at a glance the general type of furniture in use at any particular period. Thus, someone who has, say, a mid-seventeenth century table will be able to see the type of chair that might have been used with it. It should be noted, however, that the items shown are merely generally representative of their periods. There were in fact many other types in use. Thus on page 91, chairs, there are two Sheraton pieces. In reality the variety of chairs in the period was extremely wide. It would clearly be impossible to illustrate every kind of chair that was made, but those given do show characteristic features of the period.

Chairs

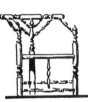

Early 16th
century
Tudor

First half 16th
century
Tudor

About 1600
Elizabethan

Early 17th
century
Early Jacobean

First half 17th
century
Jacobean

Early 17th century
Early Jacobean

Mid 17th century
Cromwellian

About 1675
Charles II

About 1690
William & Mary

Late 17th century
William & Mary

Early 18th century
Queen Anne

Early 18th century
Queen Anne

About 1735
Early Georgian

About 1755
Chippendale

About 1760
Chippendale

About 1760
Chippendale

About 1755
Chippendale

About 1765
Adam

About 1770
Hepplewhite

About 1775
Hepplewhite

About 1800
Sheraton

About 1795
Sheraton

Early 19th century
Empire

Mid 19th century
Victorian

Late 19th century
Nouveau art

Tables

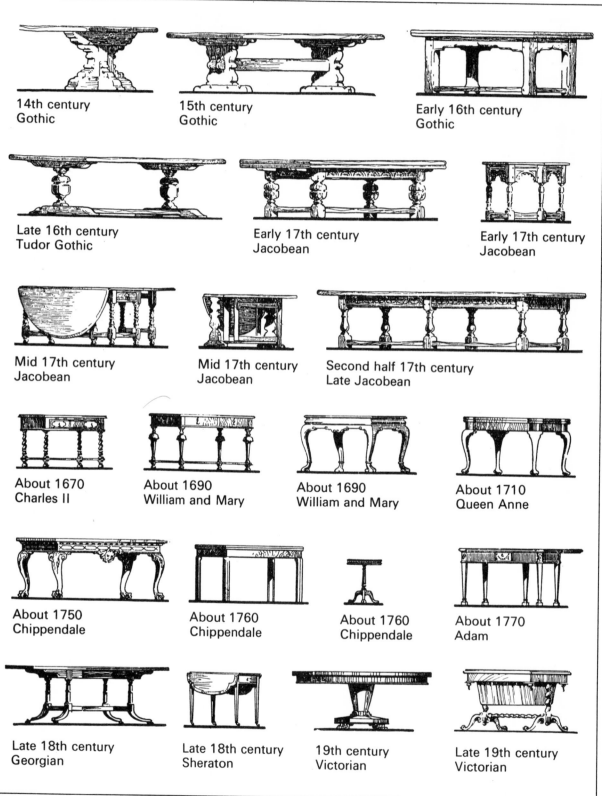

14th century
Gothic

15th century
Gothic

Early 16th century
Gothic

Late 16th century
Tudor Gothic

Early 17th century
Jacobean

Early 17th century
Jacobean

Mid 17th century
Jacobean

Mid 17th century
Jacobean

Second half 17th century
Late Jacobean

About 1670
Charles II

About 1690
William and Mary

About 1690
William and Mary

About 1710
Queen Anne

About 1750
Chippendale

About 1760
Chippendale

About 1760
Chippendale

About 1770
Adam

Late 18th century
Georgian

Late 18th century
Sheraton

19th century
Victorian

Late 19th century
Victorian

Chests

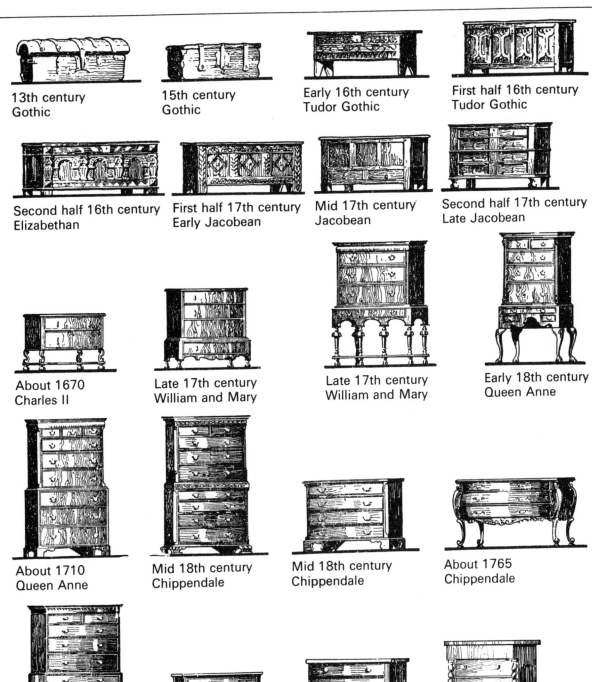

13th century
Gothic

15th century
Gothic

Early 16th century
Tudor Gothic

First half 16th century
Tudor Gothic

Second half 16th century
Elizabethan

First half 17th century
Early Jacobean

Mid 17th century
Jacobean

Second half 17th century
Late Jacobean

About 1670
Charles II

Late 17th century
William and Mary

Late 17th century
William and Mary

Early 18th century
Queen Anne

About 1710
Queen Anne

Mid 18th century
Chippendale

Mid 18th century
Chippendale

About 1765
Chippendale

About 1775
Hepplewhite

About 1790
Sheraton

19th century
Victorian

Second half 19th century
Victorian

Sideboards

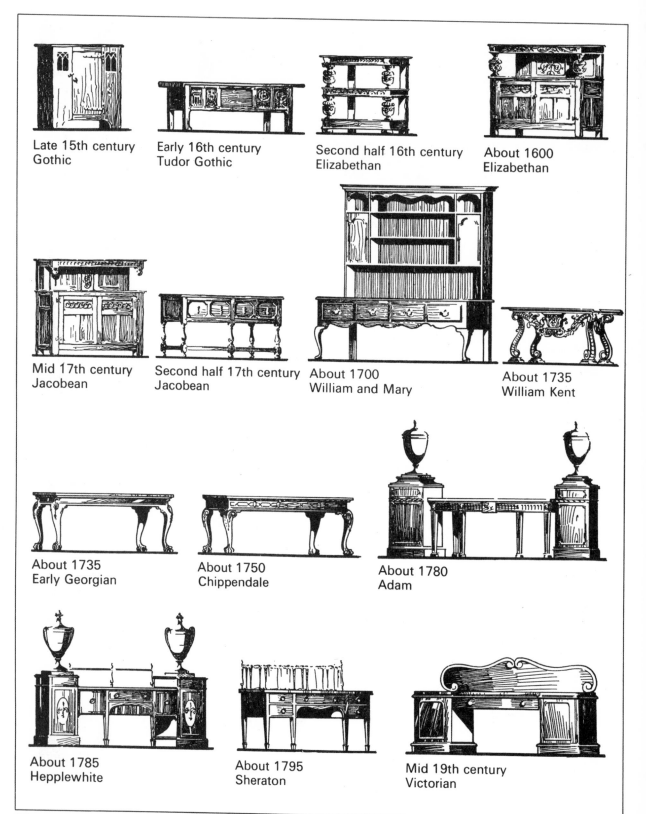

Late 15th century
Gothic

Early 16th century
Tudor Gothic

Second half 16th century
Elizabethan

About 1600
Elizabethan

Mid 17th century
Jacobean

Second half 17th century
Jacobean

About 1700
William and Mary

About 1735
William Kent

About 1735
Early Georgian

About 1750
Chippendale

About 1780
Adam

About 1785
Hepplewhite

About 1795
Sheraton

Mid 19th century
Victorian

Desks and Bureaus

17th century
Jacobean

17th century
Jacobean

Late 17th century
William and Mary

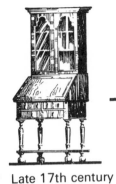

Late 17th century
William and Mary

End of 17th century
William and Mary

Late 17th century
William and Mary

Early 18th century
Queen Anne

Early 18th century
Queen Anne

Early 18th century
Queen Anne

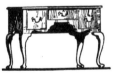

Early 18th century
Queen Anne

About 1745
Chippendale

Mid 18th century
Chippendale

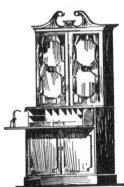

About 1770
Hepplewhite

About 1790
Sheraton

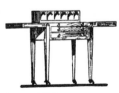

Late 18th century
Sheraton

Mid 19th century
Victorian

Early 20th century
Edwardian

Bookcases and China Cabinets

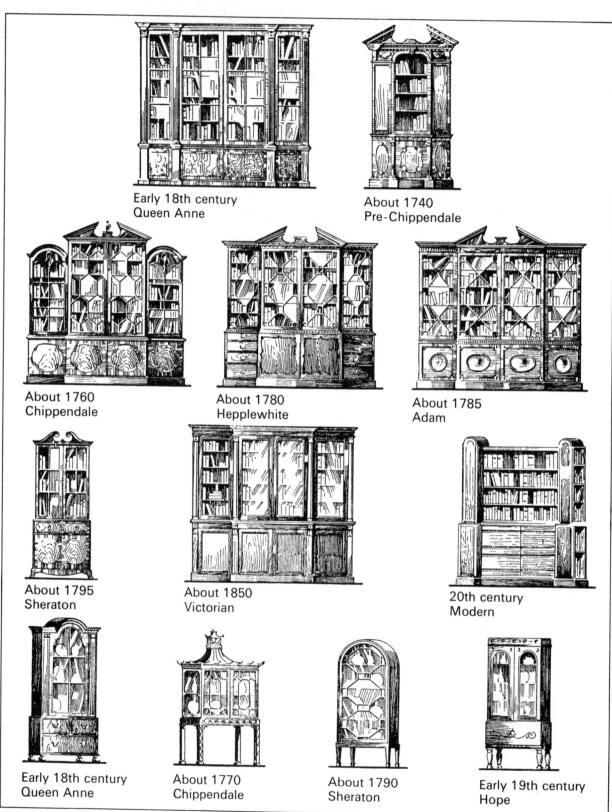

Early 18th century
Queen Anne

About 1740
Pre-Chippendale

About 1760
Chippendale

About 1780
Hepplewhite

About 1785
Adam

About 1795
Sheraton

About 1850
Victorian

20th century
Modern

Early 18th century
Queen Anne

About 1770
Chippendale

About 1790
Sheraton

Early 19th century
Hope

Bedsteads

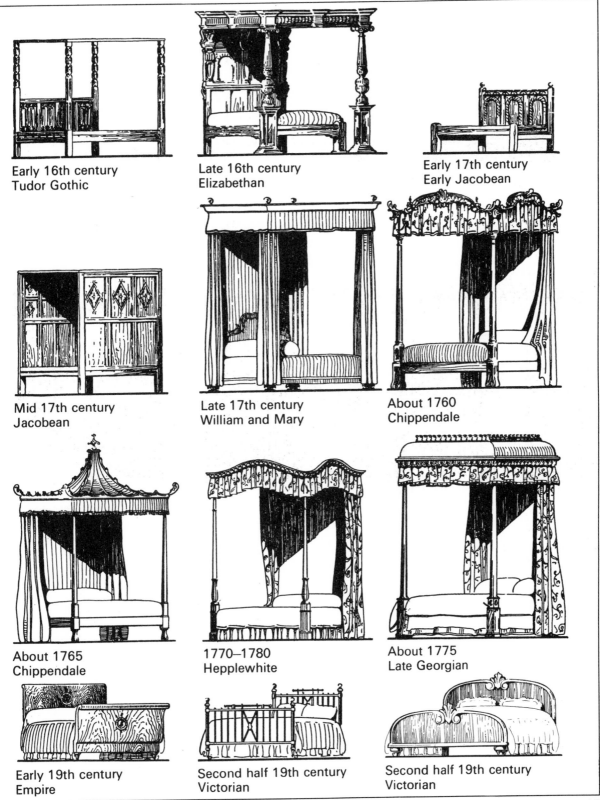

Early 16th century
Tudor Gothic

Late 16th century
Elizabethan

Early 17th century
Early Jacobean

Mid 17th century
Jacobean

Late 17th century
William and Mary

About 1760
Chippendale

About 1765
Chippendale

1770–1780
Hepplewhite

About 1775
Late Georgian

Early 19th century
Empire

Second half 19th century
Victorian

Second half 19th century
Victorian

Mouldings of the **Oak Period**

These mouldings cover roughly the period from 1500–1675. The earlier ones such as 6, 13, and 14 are Gothic in character. The others show the early influence of the Renaissance. Many of the sections and their details are quite crude, and appear to be only distantly connected with their classical origin. They suggest the work of men who received their ideas at second or even third hand. The dates given to the sections are those of the pieces from which they are taken, but it should be remembered that some of the mouldings themselves were often used with little or no change over a very long period. For instance, the rather crude rounding shown at 12 could have been used at almost any period; and the framing mouldings 24–29 are found in woodwork of both the sixteenth and seventeenth centuries.

The decoration of mouldings with carving was a favourite form of enrichment in the Elizabethan period, and during the first half of the seventeenth century. It was invariably of a deep, spirited nature, though rather crude in execution. Occasionally inlay was used, but this was generally applied to a square edge.

Nos. 1, 2, 3, 4, and 6 are cornice mouldings. Nos. 5, 7, 8, and 9 were used at eye level or rather below. Nos. 10, 11, 12, 16, 17, and 18 are from table or cabinet tops. Nos. 13, 14, 15, 21, 22, and 23 are base moulds. Nos. 19 and 20 are channellings from frame rails. Nos. 24, 25, 26, 27, 28, and 29 are edge mouldings taken from framings of panelled work.

The following are the dates of the pieces from which the mouldings are taken:
1. Late sixteenth century; 2. Early seventeenth century; 3. Seventeenth century; 4. Early seventeenth century; 5. Mid seventeenth century; 6. Early sixteenth century; 7. First half seventeenth century; 8. Early seventeenth century; 9. Mid seventeenth century; 10. Late sixteenth century; 11. First half seventeenth century; 12. Late sixteenth century; 13. Early sixteenth century; 14. Early sixteenth century; 15. Mid seventeenth century; 16. Early seventeenth century; 17. First half seventeenth century; 18. Early seventeenth century; 19. Early seventeenth century; 20. Mid sixteenth century; 21. Sixteenth century. 22. First half seventeenth century; 23. Seventeenth century; 24. Mid seventeenth century; 25. First half seventeenth century; 26. Mid seventeenth century; 27. Mid sixteenth century; 28. Late sixteenth century; 29. Early seventeenth century.

All the examples are drawn to half actual size. Many were worked with the scratch stock.

1

2

3

4

5

6

7

8

9

10

11

12

13

14

15

16

17

18

19

20

21

22

23

24

25

26

27

28

29

Mouldings of the **Walnut Period**

This relatively short period of English furniture lasted roughly from about 1660 to 1720. It was remarkable in several ways. The cabinet maker, the man who made furniture and nothing else, came into existence, superseding the carpenter who had hitherto included furniture making merely as an incidental part of his trade. Then, the craft of veneering was introduced in which the grain of the wood became a predominant feature of decoration, largely replacing carving. This resulted in considerable changes in construction, but its chief effect, so far as the present question is concerned, was that it involved the use of flat surfaces in which colour and the grain of the wood were essential features rather than shadows caused by an undulating surface, as in carving. It was rather like a picture which is painted on a flat surface. Thus finely figured woods, halved and quartered panels, cross-banding, marquetry, and so on became popular. The fashion spread even to the mouldings so that, instead of the grain running along the length, it ran crosswise. Notes

on how these mouldings were made are given on page 108.

Of the mouldings shown in the plate Nos. 1–8 are cornices of varying sizes. No. 7 is interesting in that it shows the bowed frieze so popular in the period. Sur-base mouldings are given in Nos. 9–11, used in positions rather below the eye level. Nos. 12–17 are sections used for table tops and in similar positions. Base mouldings are given in Nos. 18–21. Nos. 22 and 23 are used for barred doors. These were cross-grained and to stiffen them they were made as in Fig. 28, page 108. The walnut was prepared in a length, the grain running crosswise, and as many pieces as were needed to make the length were glued together side by side. One side was veneered as at (A), the grain running along the length. This became the underside, and the section was worked as at (B), the moulding being afterwards cut away. No. 24 is a closing mould used in the middle of a pair of doors. Nos. 25 and 26 are mirror frame sections.

Drawn half size

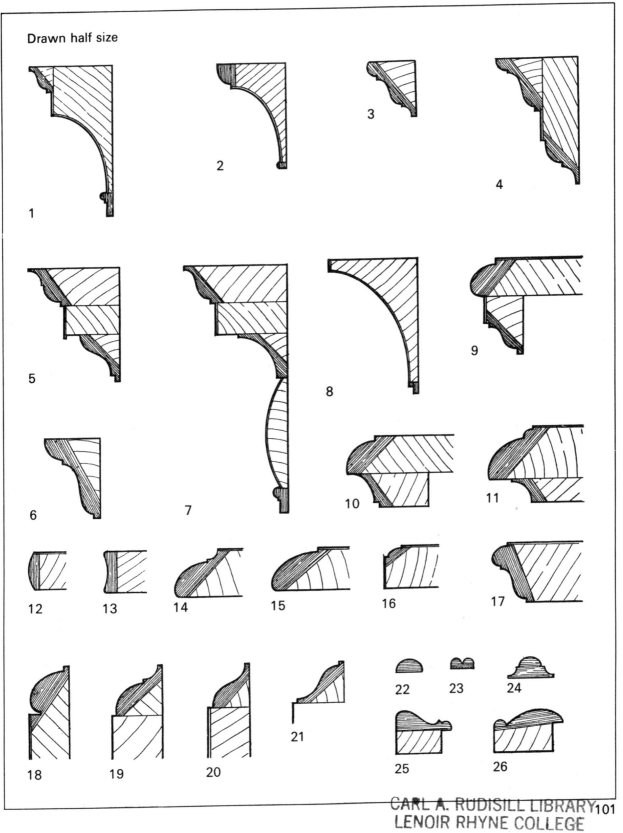

1

2

3

4

5

6

7

8

9

10

11

12

13

14

15

16

17

18

19

20

21

22

23

24

25

26

Mouldings of the **Chippendale Period**

The sections shown are taken partly from old furniture, and partly from Chippendale's *Gentleman and Cabinet Maker's Director.* Mouldings of the period were mostly founded upon classical sections, but a certain amount of simplification was inevitable because to scale down, say, a Greek or Roman entablature would result in some members being too small for practical working, and in any case the whole would look too intricate and restless. Certain members were frequently carved, the detail often being a simplification of the classical originals. Sections 1–14 are cornice mouldings, most of them being above eye level, though Nos. 9, 10, 11, and 12 would be used for a relatively low item at about eye level. Nos. 15–18 show sections of table tops and similar parts with their frieze rails beneath. Other table or low cabinet tops are given in Nos. 19–22. Sur-base mouldings are shown in Nos. 23–26. Base mouldings such as might be used for plinths, etc. are Nos. 27–33. Nos. 34–36 are small sections used in various positions—panels, frame edgings, etc. Larger mouldings were frequently built up in layers. Others were backed by softwood, the joint running at an angle roughly in line with the slope of the moulding. The cabinet maker had a range of moulding planes for working certain

stock members, and this no doubt accounts for much of the conservatism in the sections used. On the other hand many of the mouldings were worked with the scratch stock which could be fitted with cutters of any practicable shape. These cutters required nothing more than a file to fashion them. It seems, too, that carved mouldings on curved edges were sometimes worked entirely by the wood carver with gouges. This is suggested by the variation in section to be found in different parts of the same moulding. No wide variation would occur in a moulding worked with the scratch stock. In mouldings having dentils (1, 2, 3, 9, and 10) the detail might be cut in the solid, or the rebate worked extra deep and a fretted strip applied. The former was the more satisfactory method. Table tops were frequently given a thick appearance by gluing on a thicknessing beneath (19, 20, 21, 22). It had the advantage of economising in timber, and avoiding extreme weight.
All mouldings were frequently carved with conventional leafwork and other details, particularly table top, surbase, and base mouldings. Popular motifs were ribbon-and-leaf carving, nulling, acanthus leafage, bead and berry, Greek Key, and repeat cabochon pattern, occasionally frets were used.

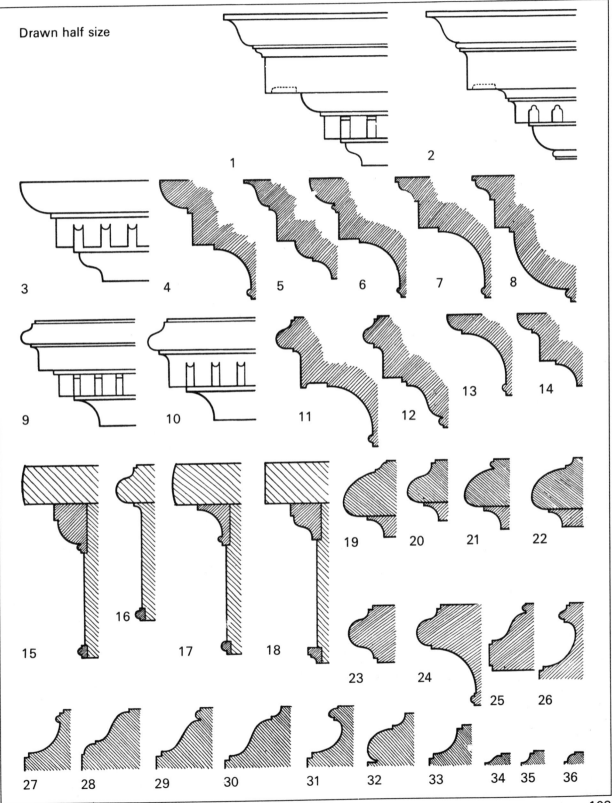

Drawn half size

1

2

3

4

5

6

7

8

9

10

11

12

13

14

15

16

17

18

19

20

21

22

23

24

25

26

27

28

29

30

31

32

33

34

35

36

Mouldings of the Hepplewhite Period

Some sections are taken from Hepplewhite's Cabinet-Maker and Upholsterer's guide, the others from old pieces. In his book Hepplewhite says in his preface '—though our drawings are all new, yet, as we designedly followed the latest or most prevailing fashion only, purposely omitting such articles whose recommendation was mere novelty, and perhaps a violation of all established rule —'. This suggests that most of them and their details are simply representative of what fashionable cabinet makers were turning out at the period. Thus the term Hepplewhite may be said to refer to a general style of furniture popular from about 1760–90, rather than suggest that a piece was the product of his workshop. Much the same may be said of the other notables of the eighteenth century.

Generally mouldings were of a refined character, and more delicate than those of the Chippendale period. Nos. 1–12 are cornice mouldings. Dentils, where they occur might be either cut in the solid or applied. In No. 12 the large cut-away hollow member is usually made separately and applied. Today it would be polished beforehand together with the main moulding to enable a clean finish to be obtained, the polish being scraped away locally where glue has to be applied. The bottom details are turnings, these consisting of two thicknesses glued together with paper in the joint, and separated after turning. At the corner the turning is a single thickness with a quadrant cut out. Frequently the turned details were in ivory. No. 13 is a typical frieze mould. Nos. 14–20 show table top or sur-base mouldings, and Nos. 21–25 base mouldings. Mouldings around table tops were sometimes carved in various conventional designs, especially when of rounded form, and flutes were frequently cut in flat members. Much Hepplewhite furniture had square-edged tops, however, frequently cross-veneered with inlay strings at the corners. Methods of construction were much as in Chippendale mouldings. Depending upon the section, cornice mouldings might be built up in layers, or they might be cut from a facing of hardwood upon a backing of softwood.

Drawn half size

1

2

3

4

5

6

7

8

9

10

11

12

13

14

15

16

17

18

19

20

21

22

23

24

25

Mouldings of the Sheraton Period

Sections were invariably delicate and refined. Generally they were not carved, though classical details or adaptations of them were sometimes used. Dentils might be either cut in the solid or applied. Small half-ball details, such as that in No. 2, would generally be cut in the solid, the carver using a gouge of the same curvature as the ball and bearing it over to follow the curve. Larger circular details such as those in No. 4 would be applied. Sometimes the dentil effect was obtained by inlaying various woods rather than by cutting the pattern in the solid wood. Nos. 1–13 are cornice mouldings. Of these Nos. 7, 9, and 11 are for low cornices at about eye level. Nos. 14–17 are sur-base sections. Table top and similar parts have sections as Nos. 18–21. Nos. 22–25 are taken from bases such as plinths. Barred door mouldings are given in Nos. 26–28. No. 29 is a shelf mould. Sheraton cornice mouldings usually consist of a facing of show wood glued to a backing of softwood. In fact in one of his books he gives exact instructions for working the mouldings with hand tools.

As a rule sideboard and similar tops were square-edged and veneered, usually cross-grain. An inlay line was frequently let in at the corners, and, apart from its decorative value, served to protect the edges of the veneer. Since these sideboard tops were frequently thick, $1\frac{1}{4}$ in. or so, they were usually in softwood with veneer at the top. In some cases, instead of the edge being veneered, it had a facing of hardwood about $\frac{1}{4}$ in. thick, invariably cross-grained, and a flat rounded section was worked in this. Although some sections seemed to remain constant over many years, some of the finer mouldings of the style would need different planes from those used for, say, Chippendale mouldings. It would have been impossible for every bench hand to have a complete range of planes. They would have the stock basic tools, and probably a few everyday moulding planes— rounds, hollows, beads, etc., but it is a fair assumption that only the fashionable master cabinet maker could have ordered fresh planes to suit the new sections. It is partly this that accounts for the difference between furniture made by a good-class firm compared with that of a jobbing cabinet maker.

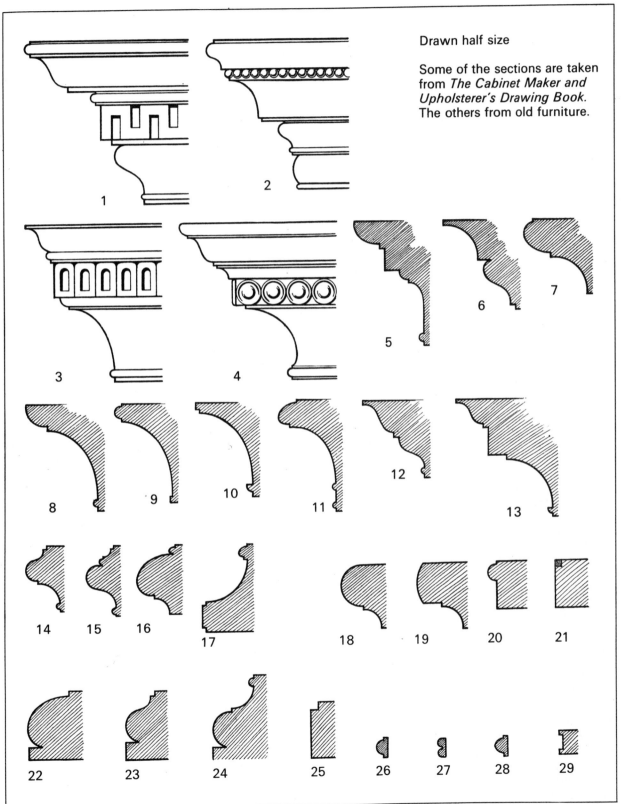

Drawn half size

Some of the sections are taken from *The Cabinet Maker and Upholsterer's Drawing Book*. The others from old furniture.

1

2

3

4

5

6

7

8

9

10

11

12

13

14

15

16

17

18

19

20

21

22

23

24

25

26

27

28

29

Construction of Walnut Mouldings

In making cross-grained walnut mouldings it will be realised that it would not have been practicable to have thick pieces of cross-grained wood, because there would be trouble due to shrinkage. The craftsmen got over the difficulty in two ways, the choice depending upon the particular section and its size. Flat, square members could be veneered, and even the larger shaped ones; the other sections were built up on a groundwork of straight-grained wood (usually pine) and a thin surface of walnut with the grain running crosswise glued on the face as in Fig. 26A. The sections on page 101 show this and it will be seen that the joint of the applied parts was made to run roughly parallel with the general slope of the moulding so that the normal grain (as distinct from end grain) was revealed on the bulk of the section. The moulding was worked in them as at B, Fig. 26.

It may be wondered how this got over the shrinkage difficulty. In fact it did not entirely do so, as an examination of some of these pieces shows, but the worst effects were minimised by drying out the thin walnut applied pieces before gluing them down on to the groundwork. The fact that the walnut was relatively thin helped in that there was a certain amount of elasticity. In the case of large mouldings, however, a common practice was to leave the glued-on pieces for as long as possible before finishing. Any joints which opened were enlarged by running a saw down them, and a piece of veneer glued in the kerf as in Fig. 27.

In the case of a table top the application depended upon the section. At A and B Fig. 26, for instance, the entire edge is moulded, and the joint of the walnut slopes. At C, the walnut is let into a rebate since only the top is moulded.

Fig. 26. How cross-grained moulding was formed by applying a strip to the edge. A shows cross-grained strip glued on, and B how it is shaped. At C is the method of forming an ogee shape with square front edge.

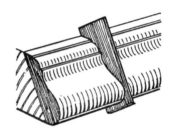

Fig. 27. Veneer glued in joint which has opened owing to shrinkage

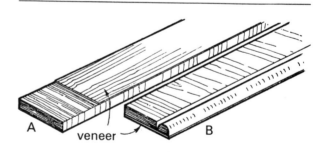

Fig. 28. How cross-grained moulding of barred door is formed. Cross-grained wood is veneered as at A, and bead worked as at B

Cabriole Legs
Setting out and making

These occur so often in furniture of the late seventeenth and the eighteenth centuries that we give the general method of setting out and the practical work involved. It is a matter of some importance, because, whereas a well-made leg is a joy to look at, a bad one is awful; bandy, ill-proportioned, and ugly. To see an example of a supremely well-made leg, dignified and graceful, turn to page 43. In the drawing it is seen from the front and side only, but in the actual chair it looks well from every angle.

Main shape

In accordance with the particular period the shape of the leg varies somewhat, but in all cases observe the following. Keep the knee high and avoid excessive shaping which suggests bandiness. In the examples in Figs. 31 and 33 it will be seen that the line beneath the knee is nearly straight. Allow the leg to taper progressively from knee to ankle. In the case of carved parts such as the shell, etc. in Fig. 32 and the ball and claw in Fig. 33 the detail is ignored at the early stage, but the line must be drawn full enough at these parts to allow enough wood for the carving. The foot may vary; the turned club foot, Fig. 31; claw and ball, Fig. 33; hoof foot (William and Mary); lion's paw (Georgian); scrolled foot; and spade foot. The procedure is the same for all, except that the club foot is turned before the shape is cut (Fig. 30).

The leg is cut from a square of timber and the only way to obtain a balanced shape is to set it out on two adjacent faces and saw through at right angles. It is obvious then that the shape

required for setting out is that of the leg seen from exactly in front.

It is desirable to bear in mind the standard size of squares available from which the shape can be cut. As a general guide, dining table legs can be cut from 4 in. squares, chair legs need $2\frac{1}{2}$ in. to 3 in. squares according to the design, and smaller legs require a thickness up to about $2\frac{1}{2}$ in. The shape needs to be kept well within these limits, however, because the sizes are nominal. The squares finish less.

As a practical example, take the table leg in Fig. 31. It is cut from a 4 in. square, the ears being extra. On a piece of thin plywood, the width of which exactly equals the size of the wood to be used, mark in lines showing the size of the top square. This particular leg has a turned club foot, and the height of this can be put in also. Now sketch in the shapes. Make good sweeping curves free from lumpiness, and avoid any suggestion of bandiness (a low knee invariable causes this). If the legs shown here are being copied, the design can be set out in squares, map fashion, but even here be sure to draw in a sweeping curve as it is easy to miss the spirit of the line when making a mechanical copy. If there is to be any carving sketch in this, remembering that in the case of knee decoration such as the shell and husk in Fig. 32 it will point towards the corner. The outline for cutting will include any projections occasioned by such carving. In the case of a carved claw-and-ball foot, such as that in Fig. 33, there are four claws spaced out as shown in the plan section (A–A). It is advisable to draw in this plan as a guide to drawing in the claws.

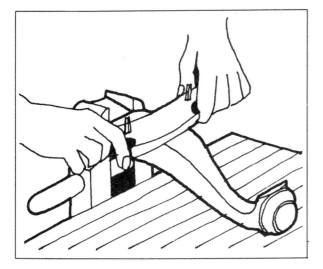

Fig. 29. Shaping with the spoke-shave. Chair-makers frequently use a scraper spokeshave which has an upright cutter. It is less liable to tear out the grain.

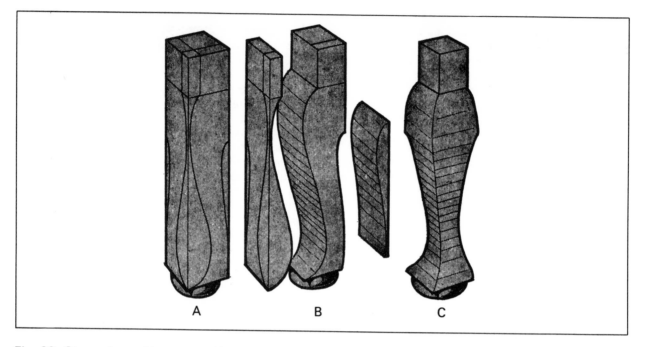

Fig. 30. Stages in marking out and sawing

Marking out

When the lines have been drawn in satisfactorily the plywood should be cut to form a templet. This can be laid on the square, first one side and then that adjacent to it, and a sharp pencil drawn around the edge as shown at (A) Fig. 30. Note that the two knees point towards each other. If the foot is of the turned club form in Fig. 31 the turning now follows, the centres being exactly in the middle at the ends. The bottom fillet and the lower shape are turned, and at the top the merest incision is made to enable the foot to finish at the same level all round. It is impossible to turn the upper part of the foot. This must be worked by hand. A, Fig. 30, shows the work after turning.

Now follows the cutting out. If a band saw is available this gives the ideal method of cutting; otherwise a chair-maker's saw, which is like a large bowsaw, should be used. Cut square through the wood to both lines as shown at (B) Fig. 30. This, of course, automatically removes the marking out on the adjacent side, and it is necessary to replace the waste pieces temporarily so that the remaining cuts in the other direction can be made. In the case of bandsawing, the lower piece when replaced acts as a support and keeps the wood square. Thumbscrews or handscrews can be used to hold

the waste piece in position, or nails can be driven into the parts to be cut away. (C), Fig. 30, shows the leg after cuts in both directions have been made.

The cleaning up can be done for the greater part with the spokeshave as shown in Fig. 29. The important point is to keep the whole balanced, and it helps in this respect if, when a few shavings are taken off at one side, the corresponding side is treated similarly. At the turned foot (Fig. 31) the corners have to be trimmed back so that the leg flows up from the turning in a clean sweep. Note specially the sections at the various heights. At the ankle it is circular, but this gradually changes to a more angular shape until at the knee it is practically a square with the corners rounded over. Practically the whole of this work can be done with the spokeshave. This will reduce the leg practically to shape, but there will be a series of flats over the entire surface caused by the tool. A wood file is used to get rid of these, being used with a rocking movement diagonally across the leg. Finish with a scraper and glasspaper. When a set of legs is being made always bring all four up to the same stage. Thus after sawing them take off the front corners of each, and so on. Do not complete one leg as it may be difficult to match the others to it.

110

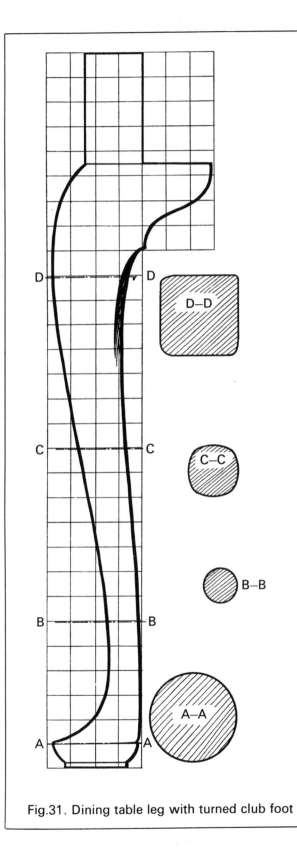

Fig.31. Dining table leg with turned club foot

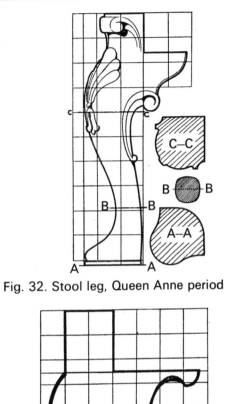

Fig. 32. Stool leg, Queen Anne period

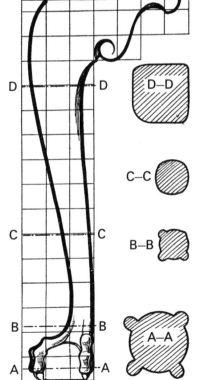

Fig. 33. Chair leg with claw and ball foot

Index